CLOUD PEAK WILDERNESS

TRAIL GUIDE, HISTORY & PHOTO ODYSSEY

M. MELIUS

TENSLEEP PUBLICATIONS

Pierre, South Dakota

Second Edition
Copyright © 1993 by M. Melius
Originally published as *Cloud Peak Primitive Area: Trail Guide, History & Photo Odyssey*.

All rights reserved. Printed in the United States of America

No part of this book may be reproduced or transmitted in any form or by any means, electronic or mechanical, including photocopying, recording or by any information storage and retrieval system now known or to be invented without permission in writing from the publisher, except by a reviewer who wishes to quote brief passages in connection with a review written for inclusion in a magazine, newspaper or broadcast.

Library of Congress Number 93-60487

ISBN 0-937603-12-0

Grateful acknowledgment is made to Harold Ober Associates for permission to reprint aphorisms from *VOICES* by Antonio Porchia, translation by W. S. Merwin, (Big Table Publishing Co., Chicago) Copyright © 1969 by W. S. Merwin.

Topographic map sections are provided by courtesy of the United States Geological Survey. Several photographs are courtesy of the U.S. Forest Service.

Published in the United States by:

Tensleep Publications
118 River Road
Pierre, SD 57501
1-800-882-5171

Copies of this book may be ordered for $14.00 postpaid.

CLOUD PEAK WILDERNESS

News For This Second Edition

The first edition of this book was published in May, 1984. In October of that year the Wyoming Wilderness Act became law. Among the wilderness areas that it designated was the Cloud Peak Wilderness, a change of name from the outdated "Primitive Area." The size of the Area also was changed, expanding from 131,000 acres to 195,000 acres. While the boundaries throughout the Area were moved outward, the greatest gain was along the east side, especially in the Little Goose Creek watershed in the northeast. The map on pp. 16-17 shows the current outline of the wilderness.

In the first edition there were many references to the "Primitive Area." These are so numerous as to preclude changing without a complete resetting of the book's text. Think "Wilderness" whenever you read "Primitive."

In the dry summer of 1988, lightning ignited a fire on the east slope of the Bighorn Mountains. The fire, dubbed the Lost Fire, began on August 14 and burned some 13,100 acres before being brought under control. The outline of the burned area is roughly circular, almost all of it in the Clear Creek watershed. Soldier Park is just to the north of the main fire area, Sherd Lake is to the south, Seven Brothers Lakes are west and Schoolhouse Park is east. (See maps on pages 44 and 55.) About half of the Lost Fire was in the wilderness.

Within the area affected by the fire about 60% actually burned. The remainder burned little if any, leaving a mosaic pattern of burned and unburned sites. By now the area has rejuvenated well, with meadows regrowing first. Forested sites have sprouted lodgepole pine by the millions, as the fire released seeds otherwise locked in cones. But charred remnants of the fire will persist for years to come. Standing dead trees may fall at anytime. The Forest Service is concentrating on the burn area to keep the trails open. Off-trail travel can be difficult, especially with a horse, as the ground is soft and spongy-wet in many places.

Human use of the Cloud Peak Wilderness has increased steadily since the 1970's. This includes both hikers and horseback riders. Facing this reality, the Bighorn National Forest in 1993 began the development of a "Cloud Peak Wilderness Schedule." The public is being invited to help determine the needs and goals for managing the wilderness. The overall goals are "to manage human use and influence so as not to alter natural processes" and "to protect an enduring resource for future generations."

How much use can the wilderness withstand? What will change, what essence of the place will be lost in the presence of so many uninvited guests? As more people visit the area it becomes more critical for each individual to feel significant, to respect the land and respect other visitors. It means being in a place with the least intruding presence, from your footprints and seated self to your odor that only you can't detect. Reducing your presence is quite a challenge, but it ought to be a wilderness skill on a par with any other--surviving a thunderstorm above timberline—immaterial to lightning—.

Some 15 campsites in the wilderness have been closed due to overuse. There are seven closures along North Clear Creek, four at Seven Brothers Lakes, and one each at Elk, Sherd, Old Crow, and Lame Deer Lakes. These sites are marked on maps here with a ⌀ symbol.

The Forest Service is encouraging would-be wilderness visitors to enjoy other places in the Bighorns instead. There are places, especially north of the wilderness, that provide people with the experiences found in wilderness, albeit below timberline: soul-stirring landforms, native wild life, defiant weather, long trails, hunting, fishing, solitude and serenity. The situation is enhanced by travel restrictions set in place by the Forest Service, which restrict motorized travel to main roads in much of the Forest. The "Travel Map" shows these restrictions and is available from any Ranger District Office.

Some of the recommended places are (from NW to SE in the Forest):

> Devil's Canyon and Bucking Mule Falls
> Lick Creek, Lake Creek, and the Dry Fork
>   of the Little Bighorn River
> Walker Creek and Walker Prairie
> Rock Creek

Except for routine trail work and improvements, no great changes have been made in the trail routes described in these pages. The Mistymoon Trail north from West Tensleep Lake is still heavily used; the Bald Ridge Trail is recommended as an alternative (see page 37). Battle Park Trailhead (p. 18) now has a well for drinking water. Rehabilitation is in the works for the popular Hunter Corrals Trailhead (p. 19). Campsites are planned near the trailhead, to be targetted for horseback users.

Corrections in the text:

> P. 3, line 11: snow accumulates <u>than</u> melts away
> P. 13, line 5: <u>clumsiness</u>
> P. 22, line 5: to Solitude <u>in</u> 6.5 miles
>   line 18: marshy and <u>as</u> heavily
> P. 61, line 16: These <u>14</u> miles

| one peak
| many valleys

Acknowledgments

Many individuals provided valuable help in compiling this guide. The author and the publisher wish to thank Edward L. Schultz, Supervisor of the Bighorn National Forest, and the following Forest Service personnel for their support and conscientious guidance: Michael Diem, Nancy Feakes, Fred Fichtner, Jim Furnish, Harold Golden, Mark Kelley, Karl Kuckuchka, Bill Nelson, Jim Powers, JT Richer, Michael Strohbusch, Brian Vachowski and Gil Walker.

The majority of the historical information included in this guide was provided through the research of Sharon Lass Field and Helen Graham. Thelma Crown, Patty Myers and Karen Mydland assisted in related research efforts. We gratefully acknowledge the contributions made by these individuals. We also appreciate the fishing information supplied by John Mueller and Louis Pechacek, Area Fisheries Supervisors for the Wyoming Game and Fish Department.

For their photographic contributions, advice and encouragement we thank Randy Brich, Pete Carrels, JoAnn Emerson and Marcus Johnshoy. In addition, we are indebted to Elsa Spear Byron, Jay Eyre, Jeff Fladeboe, Ed Lachowicz and George and Diane Prisbe for their seasoned technical assistance.

Finally, we express our gratitude to the many individuals and groups whose efforts, over a period of many years, have preserved the Cloud Peak Primitive Area.

Contents

Introduction   1
History   2
Ethical considerations...   7
Using this guide   10
Safety   12
Weather   15
Access - Trailheads   18
          Map   16-17
Trails   21
Battle Park Trailhead to Lake Solitude and Mistymoon Lake   22
 Map   28
Paint Rock Trailhead to Mistymoon Lake via Lily Lake   26
                                                Map   28
Cloud Peak and the Wilderness Basin   29
                       Map   32
West Tensleep Trailhead to Mistymoon Lake   33
                              Map   37
West Tensleep Trailhead to Lost Twin Lakes   38
                                Map   40
Circle Park Trailhead to Sherd Lake Loop   41
                       Side Trails   42
                            Map   44
Hunter Corrals Trailhead to Seven Brothers Lakes   43
                                        Map   55
Seven Brothers to Lake Angeline   48
                        Map   55
Hunter Corrals Trailhead to Mistymoon Lake   50
                                Maps   55-56
Color plates, captions and credits follow page 56
Elk Lake Loop   57
       Maps   59-60
Cross Creek Trailhead to Highland Park, Spear Lake and Elk Lake   61
   Maps   68-70
Big Goose Trailhead to Geddes Lake   71
                            Map   73
Twin Lakes Trailhead to Coney Lake   74
                            Map   75
Lower Paint Rock Trailhead to Cliff Lake, Lake Geneva and Edelman Trailhead   76
                 Side Trails   82
                        Maps   86-89
Appendix
   Loop Routes   90
   Wildlife and Fish   91
   Bird Life   93
   Resources   94
   Annotated Bibliography
   Index

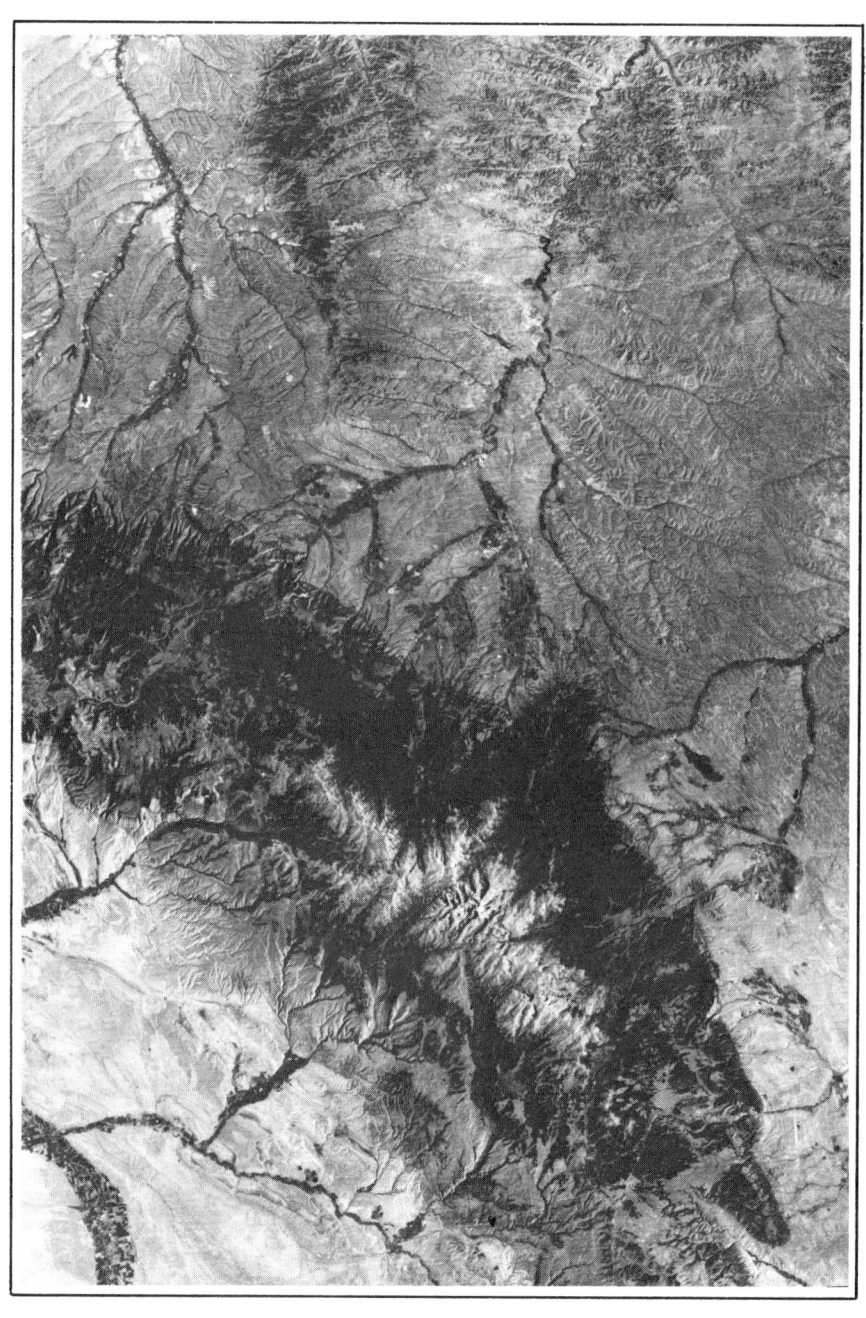

Landsat Satellite Imagery, Bighorn Range
August 11, 1977

*Photo courtesy of EROS Data Center
Sioux Falls, South Dakota*

Introduction

The Bighorn Mountains are an island of rock rising from, and eroding to, the ancient, sea-leveled plains of north central Wyoming. Their highest, central ridge is preserved within the Cloud Peak Primitive Area, where the presence of humans is limited to travel on foot or horseback only. Visitors who leave behind the comforts of contemporary society to explore the over 100 miles of trails are treated to a test of their physical state, self-reliance, and ability to adjust to the conditions the mountains impose: clear and cold, trout-perfect streams; the calls of chickadees, coyotes and elk; a taste of fresh snow in July; and the rare, cathedral air surrounding the tallest peaks.

This guide book is designed to help those who enter the Primitive Area and travel its length and width. History is provided to enable readers to appreciate how events have created and transformed the land within and around the Area. Photographs are included to give a visual sense of the various land and life forms at different seasons, in different lights.

This book is a tribute to the Cloud Peak Primitive Area, a place where we are but visitors, guests who have no physical need to be there - unlike the plants and animals who live there, whose lifeblood courses with the streams. Thus we present two contradictory invitations: to go, experience this wilderness firsthand - and to leave it alone, content with knowing it's there.

Everything is like the rivers: the work of the slopes.
— Antonio Porchia

History

    For anyone willing and able to decipher the text, the Bighorn Mountains present a record of ages past, from the most recent scratchings of human beings to the very origins of the planet's surface some three billion years ago. Although the rocks of the Bighorns are that ancient, any mountains which formed subsequently have long since eroded away to a plain. This plain was then host to great seas. Alternately flooding and subsiding, each sea left a layer of mineral and organic sediments as a record of its composition.
    These cataclysms have been interrupted indefinitely by the uplift of the Rocky Mountains, including the Bighorns. Simply stated, this uplift is the crumpling and folding of this continent's western edge, as the plate it rests on drifts westward, colliding with and overriding the Pacific plate. Beginning some 80 million years ago, this process is so slow that the rock responds plastically to the forces pressing it out of shape, although fractures and faults do occur.
    The erosive action of wind and water levels the mountains all the while they're being thrust up.

Erosion carries away the softer, sea-bottom sediments first, especially from the steeper inclines. This exposes the harder granite core - a hot, fluid substance until three billion years ago, when its variegations were immortalized as cool crystal. Sedimentary rock still clings to the lower slopes, ever-eroding into colorful canyons and outcroppings.

The most dramatic erosion, by glaciers, ended only 6,000 - 9,000 years ago, with the last Ice Age. Glaciers form as the climate cools. Year after year, more snow accumulates then melts away - sometimes hundreds of feet deep. The snow turns to ice and begins a ponderous flow down a valley. This ice sheet picks up gravel and boulders as it goes, adding to its erosive potential. It gouges a V-shaped, stream-eroded valley into one with a U-shaped bottom, then leaves rocky debris along its fringes and at its terminus when it melts.

The most grandiose work of the glacier takes place in its upper reaches. There, the snow accumulates against a wall and freezes, then separates, pulling rock away from the wall as it settles. Thus the glacier cuts a sheer wall, or cirque, into the mountain, sometimes working its way uphill in steps. In each step a bowl is scooped out, and the debris deposited downhill forms a dam for a lake filled with meltwater from the receding glaciers.

In one valley or another, the Bighorns display all these signs of glaciation: the U-shaped valleys, deepened and steepened by the ice sheets; the rock rubble left in lateral and terminal moraines; striation marks etched in rock by ice-driven boulders; and the spectacular amphitheaters at the heads of valleys, often with a 'beaded string' of lakes below.

Some nineteen glaciers of varying length and depth flowed from the spine of the range during the last Ice Age. The area they covered was roughly centered around Cloud Peak, highest in the range. A small glacial remnant still persists in a deep cirque east of the peak. Such cirques catch snow and shade it, allowing perennial snowfields to exist in some places.

As the climate became warmer the glaciers melted

and receded. Life crept in right behind them and began re-organizing the surface with myriad careful variations of its inscrutable theme. Lakes began filling with sediment and drying up, progressing from bogs to meadows to forests. Weathering - mostly frost wedging - continues relentlessly, though at a slower rate than in the Ice Age. Streambed erosion is in progress throughout, as the creeks insinuate their way into the mountain range.

  HOMO SAPIENS took part in the surge of life up the thawing ridges. Early inhabitants left few deliberate markings; only the stone remnants of their tools and weapons indicate their presence here. Exceptional is the 'Medicine Wheel', in the northern part of the range. The 'wheel' is an arrangement of stones into a hub, with spokes radiating out to a rim 35 feet away. Its purpose, as well as the nature of the people who created it, have been forgotten even by legend.

  In the nineteenth century the Bighorns became part of the freshly-weaned United States of America, and changes rivaling glaciation in extent if not severity would soon take place here. Eyes of European descent gazed upon the green slopes - eyes guided by thoughts of use: first-come, first-served, winner-take-all. Fur-trappers and explorers led the way, followed by traders, prospectors, scientists, and settlers... and an army to protect them.

  Protection was needed because they were invading someone's home. The Cheyenne, Crow and Dacotah, people whose cultures centered around these mountains and their life-giving streams fought to protect them, and the plains around saw many violent clashes between the two cultures.

  By 1880 the Indians were withdrawn from the range, and the prospectors and lumbermen moved in. The Bighorns were the scene of a minor gold rush around the turn of the century, mostly in the northern part of the range. At times there were as many as 3,000 prospectors scouring the range for the yellow metal; too little was ever found to even repay their efforts. Their diggings, cabins, and debris remain in many locations.

Others turned their muscle to a different sort of mining: lumbering. Wood was needed for railroad ties, fence posts, houses, barns, saloons... Wood was needed for the flumes to carry the cut timber downslope. (One such 'wooden waterway' was 35 miles long and considered an engineering marvel in its day.) Wood was needed, or at least desired, and the taking was done with little thought of the consequences - except for the takers.

Meanwhile, ranches and farms were being started on the slopes and plains around the Bighorns. In this dry country rainfall is a limiting factor, and agricultural people looked to the mountains for a more certain water supply, mostly for irrigating alfalfa. They built ditches to carry the water and reservoirs to store it. The most ambitious project was the Cloud Peak Reservoir, constructed in the 1880's on the east slope.

As the ranches grew and available range shrank, cattle and sheep were driven in ever-greater herds to the high meadows of the Bighorns for summer pasture. Bitter disputes between ranchers over grazing rights led to overgrazing, as the stockmen tried to forcibly assert their claims to the forest lands.

In the midst of this rapid development in, and exploitation of, the mountains, the Bighorn National Forest was established by proclamation of President Cleveland on February 22, 1897. Set aside as a recreation preserve, with grazing curtailed and regulated, the range now spawned the birth of the dude ranch industry. People began to venture into the Bighorns for sightseeing, hunting and fishing. Many of the dude ranches provided pack horses and guides for these adventures.

After being designated a National Forest, the range enjoyed some tranquility as development slowed. Most construction was for recreation purposes: campgrounds, trails, and some minor roads. Construction of the Solitude Trail began in 1920.

On March 5, 1932, the establishment of the Cloud Peak Primitive Area ensured the preservation of the glacier-carved central core of the range. The

Primitive Area contains nearly 137,000 acres. With the exception of minimal trail construction and improvement, little has been done to this wilderness. The area's imaginary borders have been periodically expanded and the Primitive Area awaits re-designation as a Wilderness Area.

The ability of the forests and meadows to re-cover after lumbering, grazing, or fires have diminished them is well evidenced by photographs taken 75 years apart (1900, 1975). They show bare ridges now dark with pine and spruce, stream banks stabilized with tenacious plant roots, and rocky meadows turned fibrous and green.

And in the future? Another Ice Age would surely bring the snowcap back to the Bighorns, and send life scurrying down the slopes to await a better day. A warming trend would do the opposite. Given the vagaries of our planet's climate, it could go either way.

The areas we preserve as wilderness serve as a comparison, a 'control' - albeit barely understood - for our own potentially discordant variations of the intricate theme: sun, earth, and life. When discord could be fatal. Wilderness preserves an undisturbed record and on-going replay of the processes which beget such beings as ourselves. Without it we are guided only by our divergent viewpoints, with nothing to compare them with but the cold darkness just beyond the highest peaks.

Ethical Considerations...

At every moment we are at once coming and going. Yet so intent are we on destination that we easily forget where we have gone - like a trail: something followed but just as surely left behind.

Everything that lives and moves leaves a trail, from the most subtle scents and sounds to the deepest footprint. While other animals may be more or less carefree concerning theirs, we humans have the ability to care about our trails and to respond by minimizing them.

The most visible and persistent trails are those left by our feet. Grasses and forbs of the high country do their best given the thin soils, low available moisture, and short growing season, but they simply cannot withstand repeated trampling. Thus the first rule for wilderness visitors is: stay on the trails. Even in crossing a lovely meadow where it seems you're adding to the injury by following the trail, the alternative - walking to one side - only opens a new wound. In places where the trail has been widened by less-conscious travelers, stick to the center - unless you'd prefer more trail and less vegetation.

When you must leave the trail, try to walk on rocks - this writer's favorite mode. It allows going slower, varying your stride, and being more observant, not only of the immediate ground but also of your whole surroundings. On the trail you can easily get into a repetitive rhythm which lulls you into a sleepwalk. Rock-hopping keeps you on your toes. In some places, especially above timberline, rock is about all there is so it's no extra effort to rock-hop. Drawbacks include the greater shocks to your body, compared with the softer ground; and the fact that bare rock can be quite slippery when wet.

Less visible than foot trails but just as insidious

are the traces we leave in our body wastes. The damage occurs when run-off from snow or rain leaches through the feces, carrying disease organisms into streams and rendering their water unfit to drink without sterilization. To minimize this risk, deposit all fecal matter at least 200 feet from any body of water. Find a spot with the deepest soil and dig a hole at least 8 inches deep, covering it well when you're through.

Campsites are another highly visible and potentially damaging aspect of a wilderness excursion. Pick a secluded spot, for your benefit as well as others', well away (100 feet) from trails and water, and if possible one without vegetation. When camping with a group, camp in one area, and limit side-trips to agreed-upon routes.

A campfire is part of the romance of camping for some people, but is usually unnecessary except in extreme wet/cold or emergencies. A gas backpacking stove is cleaner, faster, and leaves no trace. In the areas where wood is scarce and precious, fires are prohibited and a stove is a necessity for cooking.

Fires should be small, use only dead and down wood, be made in a shallow pit with no rocks, and drowned out with water before being left behind. Scatter the ashes widely over good soil well away from water. Fill in the firepit, leaving it as much as possible the way you found it.

Other considerations include: Pack out all your trash. Do all your washing at least 100 feet from water. Make no unnecessary noise which disturbs the peace of other visitors as well as stressing the wildlife which lives there.

The detrimental impacts to trails and campsites can be avoided by snow camping, via skis or snowshoes. Marks left in deep snow won't persist or matter (except aesthetically). The best time for such a trek into the Bighorns is in early spring - March to May - when there's a good snow base, with milder temperatures and longer days than in winter.

The worst time, impact-wise, is in June and July, when rains and snowmelt combine to turn trails into mud or even flowing rivulets.

In short, try to become better conscious of your presence and its effects - both immediate and persistent - on the communities you pass through: the soil, plants, birds and mammals, and the air and water that unite us.

Using This Guide

The format used in this guide book clarifies the composite trail system of the Cloud Peak Primitive Area. The trail network is broken into separate trail narratives accompanied by topographic map sections. As you read the accounts, refer to the trails depicted on the topographic maps. The maps included in each section are part of a 7.5 minute quadrangle - the entire quadrangle is not shown. You'll notice that there are often several approaches to the same point, i.e. Mistymoon Lake, Highland Park.

The U.S. Forest Service has named and numbered the trails. This guide uses most of their names but not their numbering. The most frequent trail number encountered in the Primitive Area is trail #38, the Solitude Loop. The Solitude route circles the northern half of the Primitive Area.

The description of trails begins with trailheads on the SW edge of the Primitive Area. The accounts then proceed counter-clockwise around the entire area.

The trail narratives open with an overview of the trail: outstanding features it leads to, its length and elevation gain corresponding to slope, junctions with other trails, and distance to the first good drinking water (not a concern when there is snow).

The narratives describe the trail as being level, moderate or steep. These descriptions of slope are not based on difficulty (easy, strenuous) which varies from person to person and with the direction of travel. Instead, slope is derived from on-the-trail experience, looking up or down the trail, then hiking it. Where two terms are used, i.e. moderate-steep, the first condition is predominant. (Trail accounts describe a trail while traveling in one direction. If you are using the trail but coming from the opposite direction, read the account 'backwards'.)

As you use this guide you may notice that two conspicuous features are rarely mentioned. One feature, signs, aren't usually noted because they might not remain where indicated. The Forest Service provides an excellent network of descriptive signs throughout the area. Unfortunately, many of these signs are stolen. As a result, the existence of any given sign is doubtful at all times. Fortunately, tree blazes and rock cairns marking the trails aren't as likely to be removed.

Campgrounds are the other feature we mention sparingly. We have not pointed out most campgrounds shown on the topographic maps because these areas are overused. These campsites, and especially the vegetation around them, are taking a beating. We encourage you to select an unused campsite and to leave no traces of your stay.

Several 'unsanctioned' routes (e.g. Exit Pass on the Cliff Lake Loop) are noted or described. The Forest Service does not officially recognize or maintain these routes. The Forest Service calls these routes 'man-ways' - which is to say that people use them and they get made. Most of these routes are at high elevations in exposed, rugged terrain. These routes should not be used by improperly-equipped or novice hikers. As with all off-trail travel, we recommend boulder-hopping to prevent destruction of delicate vegetation.

This guide is designed to enhance your visit to the Primitive Area. To fully understand the trail system of the Cloud Peak Primitive Area, refer often to the topographic map sections as you carefully read the narratives. To augment the descriptive information in this guide, obtain complete topographic quadrangle maps.

Safety

The Bighorn Mountains present many 'moods' varying with the season, weather conditions and the state of mind of the observer. As 'state of the mind' so often depends on 'state of body' and is the only variable we can control, it is essential to prepare well for a visit to these mountains. Otherwise, their 'mood' can go from serene to threatening to deadly in a matter of hours.

General guidelines for travel in the backcountry include: (1) be prepared in terms of clothing, shelter, food and first aid equipment, (2) don't be careless, the severity of a minor mishap is magnified in the remote, rugged terrain, (3) leave your itinerary and dates of travel with someone dependable.

The safety advice that follows is not exhaustive. Educate yourself about wilderness survival, safety and first aid before entering the Primitive Area.

OVEREXERTION AND ALTITUDE SICKNESS: Acclimate yourself slowly to the altitude. The Forest Service reports that many people rush into the wilderness and climb too quickly, giving themselves altitude sickness or, in the worst cases, heart attacks. Altitude sickness is caused by dehydration, overexertion and lack of oxygen. Symptoms include nausea, dizziness, headache and loss of appetite. To treat altitude sickness, drink fluids, eat high energy foods and rest. If symptoms persist or if you or a member of your party spits up blood, develops a hacking cough or is irrational, descend to a lower elevation immediately.

HYPOTHERMIA: Caused by wind combined with

moisture, this can occur even when the air temperature is +50 degrees Fahrenheit. Hypothermia is a lowering of internal body temperatures, eventually fatal if not treated when symptoms first appear. Symptoms include uncontrollable shivering, cluminess, drowsiness and incoherence (so trust the symptoms, not the victim). Get the victim to a sheltered, dry place, exchange wet clothing for warm and dry clothing and put the victim in a sleeping bag. Give the victim warm fluids (not alcohol). If the victim is badly impaired, put him/her in a sleeping bag with another person. Both people should be stripped to speed up the transfer of body heat. Try to keep the victim awake.

To avoid hypothermia, wear rain- and wind-proof clothing and keep your body core warm with plenty of fluids and food. Hypothermia is likely to occur in cold, wet and windy weather.

LIGHTNING: As lightning occurs mostly in afternoon thunderstorms in the Bighorns, make sure you are not in high, exposed areas when storms approach. If caught in a storm, get to the lowest place you can find and remove metal pack frames.

IF YOU ARE LOST: Don't panic. Look over the maps you have and try to approximate your position with your compass. In the Primitive Area, most trails go up or down along streams and streams eventually lead down to civilization. If lost in bad weather or at nightfall, find the best shelter available and keep warm. Avoid getting wet. If injured or immobilized, make a signal fire.

STREAM CROSSINGS: At some points in the Primitive Area, the Forest Service has built sturdy bridges across deep, fast moving streams. Other streams have logs across or use exposed rocks in the streambed for crossing. Some streams must be waded. If you must wade a stream, remove your socks and put your boots back on or wear sneakers; don't cross barefoot. Face upstream for better stability and work your way sideways across the stream. Unbuckle the waist belt of your pack so you can shed it quickly should you fall into the stream. Cross slowly and deliberately using a hiking stick or tree branch for support. Streams often swell towards afternoon as snow melts above, allowing for easier crossing in the early morning.

DRINKING WATER: Some of the water in the Primitive Area may not be suitable for drinking unless purified. Giardia, a microscopic protozoa which causes intestinal distress, is carried in many streams in the Rocky Mountains. Even though the water looks clear and clean, it might contain giardia or other organisms. To purify water, several methods are available, none proven to be 100% effective. Iodine tablets, water filters or boiling water for 10 minutes are the most often used means of purifying water.

Throughout this guide we refer to sources of water that should be uncontaminated. These sources are usually springs, high remote streams, or water flowing from a steep ridge. These references to good water are based on our observations and experience in the Primitive Area; if you are unsure whether any water source is contaminated, purify the water before drinking.

WILD ANIMALS: The wildlife that still lives in the Bighorns poses little danger to people. Rattlesnakes aren't usually found above an altitude of 7,000', but be wary of the exception. Black bears do inhabit the range. These bears are rarely seen and there is little history of adverse contact between bear and man; if you spot a bear, stay away from it. Keep a clean camp and store food away from sleeping areas.

OTHER SAFETY CONSIDERATIONS: Keep your hiking party together. Watch weather closely to prevent being caught at high elevations during snow or lightning storms. If walking on snow, be aware of what's under the snow (flowing streams, lakes). Be careful with fires, stoves and fuel. Don't throw rocks or debris from high places. Don't take unnecessary chances in the wilderness.

Weather

Most of the Primitive Area is above 9,000'. In selecting shelter, clothing and sleeping bags, keep in mind that, even in the summer, evenings are chilly and nights are cold. Also, snow squalls and afternoon thundershowers can occur anytime during the summer.

The driest months are July, August and September, the wettest months are April, May and June. The east slope of the Bighorns receives more precipitation than the west slope.

With average annual snow depths of 55 to 65 inches, portions of the Primitive Area retain snow cover well into August. Long sections of trail in areas such as Florence Pass and Geneva Pass might be under snow as late as August. In the high country, be alert for avalanche dangers and be cautious if walking in areas with snow overhangs (cornices).

The following list indicates the normal daily maximum and minimum temperatures for the 9,000' level in the Bighorns. These temperature averages do not take into account extreme weather patterns, wind and humidity.

	Max. °F	Min. °F		Max. °F	Min. °F
Jan.	25	5	July	70	35
Feb.	30	10	Aug.	70	40
Mar.	35	10	Sept.	60	30
Apr.	45	20	Oct.	50	25
May	50	30	Nov.	35	15
June	65	35	Dec.	30	10

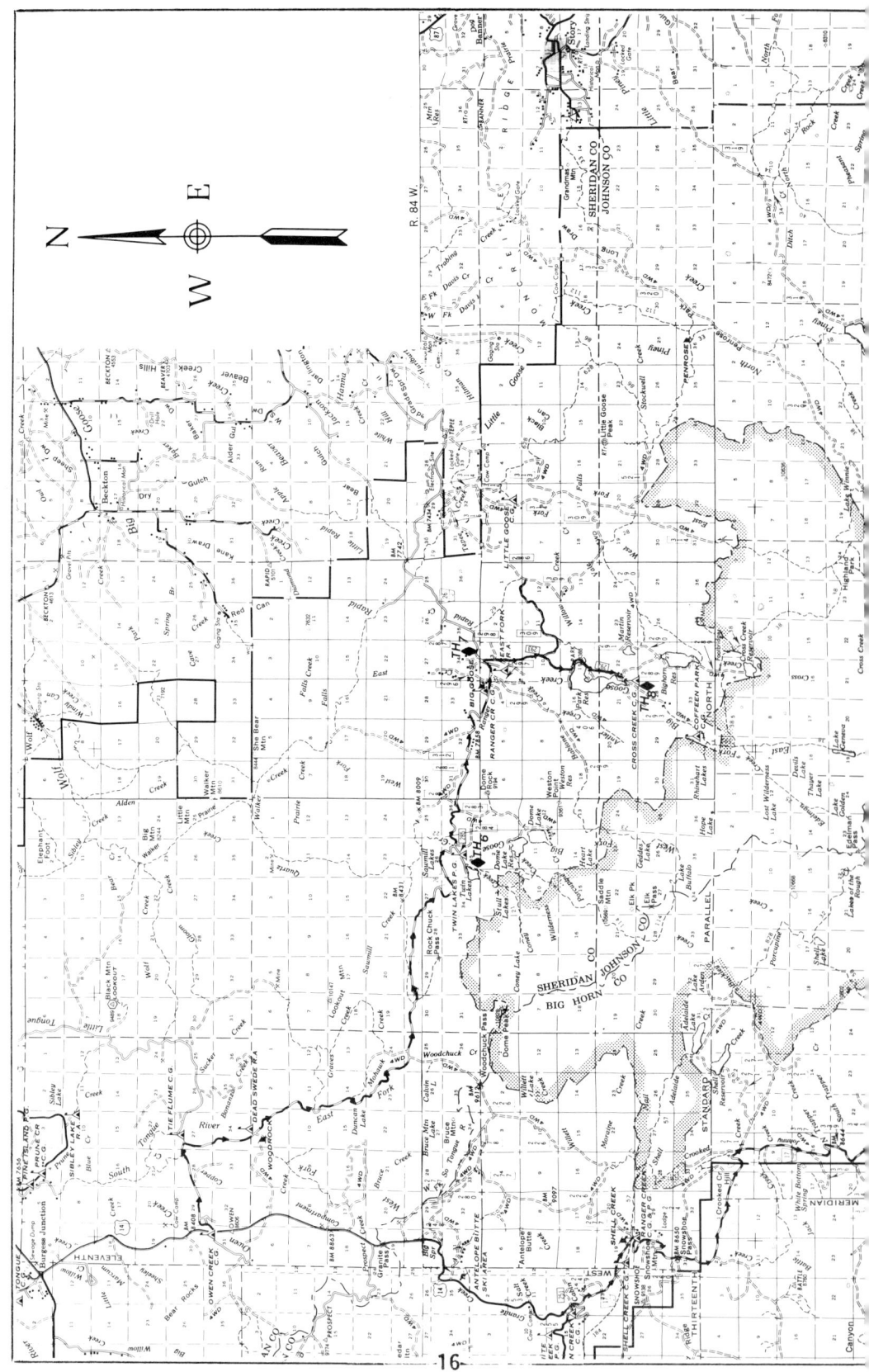

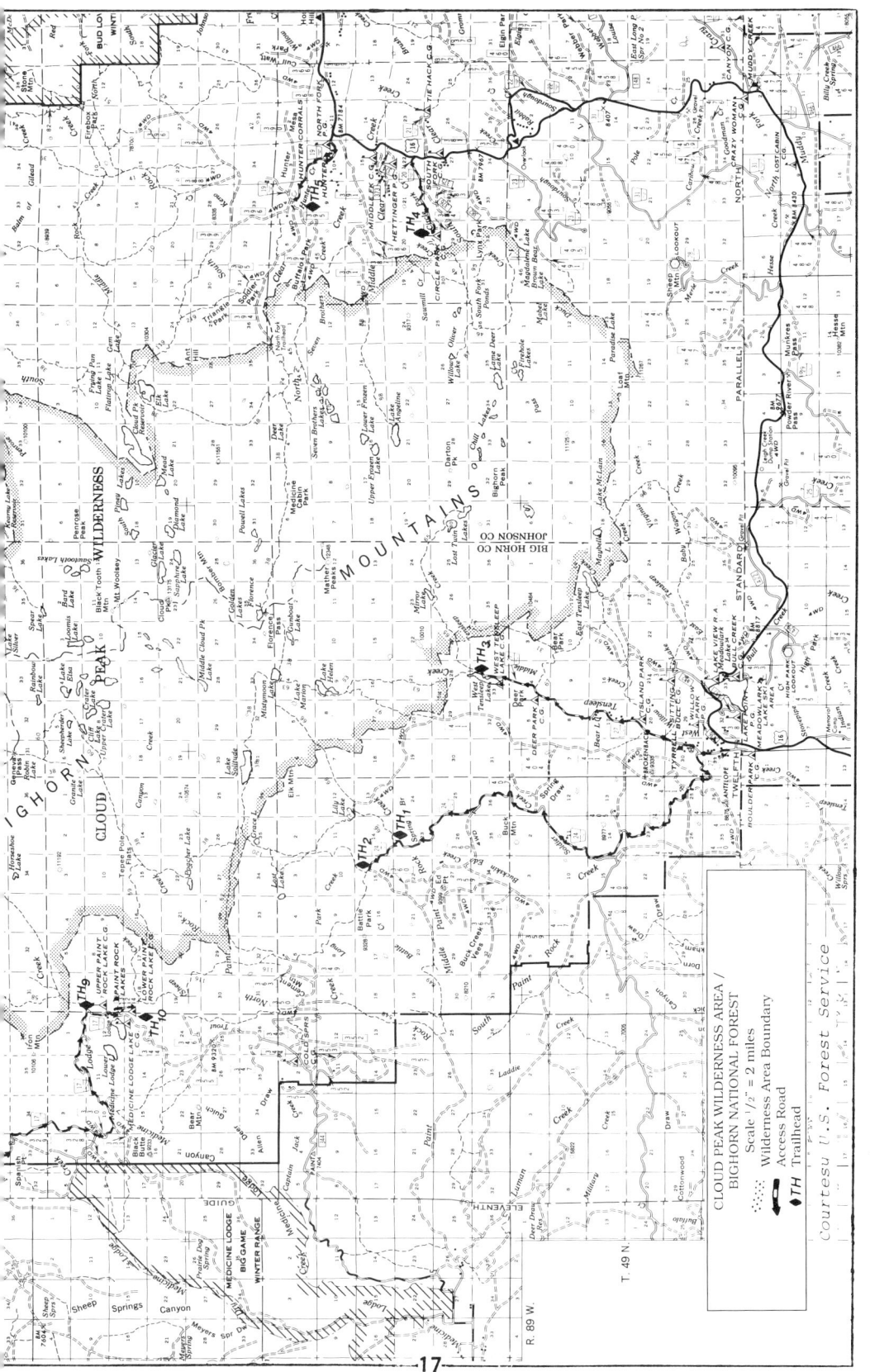

Access - Trailheads

The trailheads listed are also indicated on the Bighorn National Forest map. Although there might be several routes to a trailhead, the access roads described in this section are considered to be best suited for all vehicles including passenger cars.

PAINT ROCK TRAILHEAD (1): The turnoff for this trailhead is 20 miles NE of Tensleep, on U.S. 16 or 44 miles SW of Buffalo, on U.S. 16. The turnoff from the highway is well marked with signs indicating directions to West Tensleep Lake and Tyrell Ranger Station. Follow the all-weather Forest Service road 1 mile north to a junction, the road left leads to Paint Rock Trailhead and Battle Park Trailhead. The main road, right, heads north past Tyrell Ranger Station.

Paint Rock Trailhead is 13 miles NW of this junction on an all-weather road suitable for passenger cars. Sections of this road are rough - top speed is 25 MPH.

Located in a depression just east of the road, the trailhead does not have a large capacity. There are no horse corrals.

BATTLE PARK TRAILHEAD (2): Located 1 mile NW of Paint Rock Trailhead on same road. Battle Park has toilets, a large parking area and horse corrals.

WEST TENSLEEP LAKE TRAILHEAD (3): The turnoff for this trailhead is 20 miles NE of Tensleep on U.S. 16 or 44 miles SW of Buffalo on U.S. 16. From the turnoff, head north on a good, all-weather road for 7.5 miles. Road passes east of Tyrell Ranger Station.

The trailhead is located at road's end on the east shore of West Tensleep Lake; capacity is 45 cars.

CIRCLE PARK TRAILHEAD (4): The turnoff for Circle Park is 14.5 miles west of Buffalo on U.S. 16. The trailhead is 2.5 miles SW of U.S. 16 on a good all-weather road. Trailhead and registration box are located at the west end of Circle Park campground. Parking for horse trailers is available just before the campground.

HUNTER CORRALS TRAILHEAD (5): The Hunter Corrals turnoff is 11.5 miles west of Buffalo on U.S. 16. The trailhead is 2.5 miles west on a good, all-weather road. The road passes by the North Fork Picnic Ground and Hunter Ranger Station.

The trailhead has ample parking, a toilet and horse corrals.

TWIN LAKES TRAILHEAD (6): The turnoff for this trailhead is 34 miles SW of Dayton on U.S. 14. Twin Lakes is 15 miles SE on a good, all-weather road that passes Tie Flume and Dead Swede campgrounds. This road also leads to the Big Goose Ranger Station and Cross Creek Trailhead.

Park at the Twin Lakes Picnic Ground located 0.5 mile south of the main road.

BIG GOOSE RANGER STATION (7): The Big Goose Ranger Station is located 5 miles east of Twin Lakes Picnic Ground on the same all-weather road.

The Ranger Station should be used for parking by those who want to hike to Geddes Lake via Babione Creek. This trailhead can be used by those who don't want to drive through or leave their car in Big Goose Park to the south. If you leave your car at the Ranger Station, tell Forest Service personnel about your itinerary.

CROSS CREEK TRAILHEAD (8): To reach this trailhead, proceed east of Big Goose Ranger Station for 0.8 mile crossing the east fork of Big Goose Creek to junction. Cross Creek campground is 6 miles south of the junction on an all-weather road. Follow the circular east shoreline of Park Reservoir and continue south past Spear-O-Wigwam Resort. Cross

Creek campground is 0.4 mile south of the resort over a narrow, rocky road. The trailhead is an open area just south of the campground.

Coffeen Park is 2 miles SW of Cross Creek campground over a rough jeep road, (no vehicle travel advised). Trail south from Coffeen splits after 1 mile; trail SW is to Edelman Pass, trail south is to Lake Geneva. The road SE from Cross Creek campground, (past west shore of Bighorn Reservoir) leads to a connection with Solitude Trail SE to Highland Park.

A road SW out of Big Horn, (8 miles SW of Sheridan) also leads to Big Goose Ranger Station, Twin Lakes and Cross Creek trailheads. It's 17.5 miles from Big Horn to Big Goose Ranger Station on a road known as the 'Red Grade Road'. Although rough, this county road/Forest Service road can be traversed by passenger cars - top speed is 20 MPH.

EDELMAN TRAILHEAD (9): The access road is located 15.8 miles NE of Shell, on U.S. 14. The turnoff is marked by a sign indicating the location of Cabin Creek campground. The trailhead is 24 miles SE of U.S. 14. Passenger cars can traverse this road unless there has been heavy snow or rain.

The road is in good condition in some sections, rocky and rutted in others. Drive carefully over this road - top speed is 25 MPH.

The Edelman Trailhead is a large clearing with ample parking.

LOWER PAINT ROCK TRAILHEAD (10): 1.5 miles south of Edelman on Forest Service road. Located just north of Lower Paint Rock Lake, the trailhead has ample parking and horse corrals.

Certainties are arrived at only on foot.
— Antonio Porchia

Trails

Battle Park Trailhead to Lake Solitude and Mistymoon Lake

The trail from Battle Park enters the Primitive Area from the west and leads to the gorgeous Lake Solitude and beyond that to Mistymoon Lake and the alpine country of the Bighorn Divide. While its net rise of 150' to Solitude is 6.5 miles includes intermediate gains of 700', the trail is moderate-level throughout. Good water might be available on the south shore route of Lake Solitude.

This trail is the shortest to Lake Solitude but not the most wild, being a jeep trail for the first 3 miles. A slightly longer foot trail from the Paint Rock Trailhead via Lily Lake (p. 26) also goes to Solitude and might be preferred. The trailhead at Battle Park has camping facilities, horse corrals and ample parking space. At the west end of the park the jeep trail enters timber and heads north, crossing Battle Creek and turning NE towards Long Park. The southern part of this park is marshy and is heavily trampled by cattle as the park is grazed (1983). The jeep trail turns north into the park area, crossing Long Park Creek along the way.

Midway into Long Park the foot trail from Lily Lake may be found just to the east. About 0.5 mile from the north edge of the park the trails split, eventually rejoining south of Grace Lake. The foot trail is shorter but the jeep trail has the advantage of connecting with a spur trail to Lost Lake, 0.5 mile to the west.

The foot trail heads north out of Long Park, climbing a ridge which extends west from Elk Mountain. Midway along the moderate-steep descent to Grace Lake, the jeep trail from Lost Lake rejoins the foot trail.

Pass Grace Lake on the west and continue north, entering the Primitive Area just north of the lake. Descend into the valley of Paint Rock Creek, where a trail heading north past Poacher Lake to the North High Park Trail (p. 82) intersects. You are now on the Solitude Trail, with Lake Solitude 1 mile east.

Solitude was probably formed by a dam of glacial drift deposited at the west end of its narrow, deep basin. Nearly one mile in length, it is the largest lake in the Primitive Area aside from man-made reservoirs - a fate this lake nearly befell.

In 1943, the Bureau of Reclamation proposed plans for an earthen dam at the west end of Lake Solitude to hold irrigation water for the Bighorn Basin to the west. An access road was also proposed. After much local public debate, much of it opposed to the dam, the project was postponed indefinitely in 1948.

Follow the trail around the southern shore. The east part of the trail was laboriously built through a

Trail on south shore of Lake Solitude.
Photo by Marcus Johnshoy

great boulder field lying like a giant 3-D jigsaw puzzle between the lake and the ridge. Clean, clear water is available here, tumbling over and under the boulders from Elk Mountain to the south.

East of the lake, cross Paint Rock Creek in a large flat outwash where the creek slows and splits into several smaller channels. From here the 3 miles to Mistymoon Lake is moderate-steep as 1,200' of elevation is gained.

Paint Rock Creek, east of Lake Solitude.
Photo by Ken Melius

Proceed east along the north bank of the creek, crossing a tributary on a sturdy bridge after 0.5 mile. This tributary drains the Wilderness Basin to the NE (for description of this high, remote basin, see p. 30). Just NE of the bridge are 20' waterfalls.

Continue the moderate ascent through subalpine

terrain. The trail parallels the creek, at some points 200' above its bed. Just over 1.5 miles from Solitude, cross the creek to the south side. From here on note the views to the west, NE (Cloud Peak) and east (Bomber Mountain). Look for sunlit reflections from the wreckage of a bomber which crashed in 1943 on the then - unnamed mountain (see p. 53 for further description).

As the trail leaves the creekbed and ascends along the ridge south, look north across a bog etched with a network of sinuous channels. There, where a tributary descends to Paint Rock with a gravelly alluvial fan, is a small waterfall which marks the most accessible route to Cloud Peak (p. 29).

Now above timberline where fires are prohibited, turn south and go past several ponds. This is the division between the Paint Rock watershed and that of West Tensleep Creek. Descend to Mistymoon where trails join from the SE (Lily Lake, p. 26); south (West Tensleep, p. 33); and east (Florence Pass, p. 50).

Paint Rock Trailhead to Mistymoon Lake via Lily Lake

This trail leads to Lily Lake and from there follows Middle Paint Rock Creek up to a pass (10,550') just east of Mistymoon Lake. It is moderate with steep passages as it rises 1,600' in 6.8 miles. Good water might be available at the upper end of Middle Paint Rock Creek.

The trailhead (referred to as Paint Rock Trailhead) is on the east side of Battle Park road and is clearly indicated by a road sign. From here the well-marked trail begins a moderate-steep incline through dense, shady stands of lodgepole pine, passing wet swales along the way. After 1.5 miles emerge onto the open meadows around Lily Lake. At the south shore the trail splits. Take the right fork, going east. (Trail north is to Lake Solitude via Grace Lake. Pass the west shore of Lily, climb ridge through dense timber, descend ridge and cross south fork of Long Park Creek. Traverse a slight ridge and then cross the north fork of Long Park Creek. Enter Long Park and join trail coming south from Battle Park Trailhead.)

The small northern portion of Lily Lake is green with water lilies and drains to the south part which is sky blue and clear. The rocky mass of Elk Mountain looms to the NE.

From Lily Lake (trail splitting off south from Lily leads to Bald Ridge and down to West Tensleep Trailhead) steer east across the meadow, cross a small creek then head NE along the north side of Middle Paint Rock Creek. The meadow here is heavily grazed (1983) and has numerous cowpaths, generally leading up the drainage. Rock cairns mark the main trail.

After 0.7 mile, cross the creek and stay on the south side the rest of the way. The next 2 miles are moderate-level, through meadows and sparse timber.

The last 1.5 miles are steep. ascending the narrow rocky valley. Here the valley opens to the alpine terrain west of Mistymoon Lake. A small, unnamed lake adorns the passage between ridges rising 500' to the south and NW where you turn east to descend to Mistymoon.

Open fires are not permitted in this area or in any similar alpine area in the Bighorns. Bring a stove for cooking.

At Mistymoon the trail intersects the Solitude Trail going north to Lake Solitude (p. 22), or the Cloud Peak climb (p. 29), south to West Tensleep Creek (p. 33) and Florence Pass (p. 50).

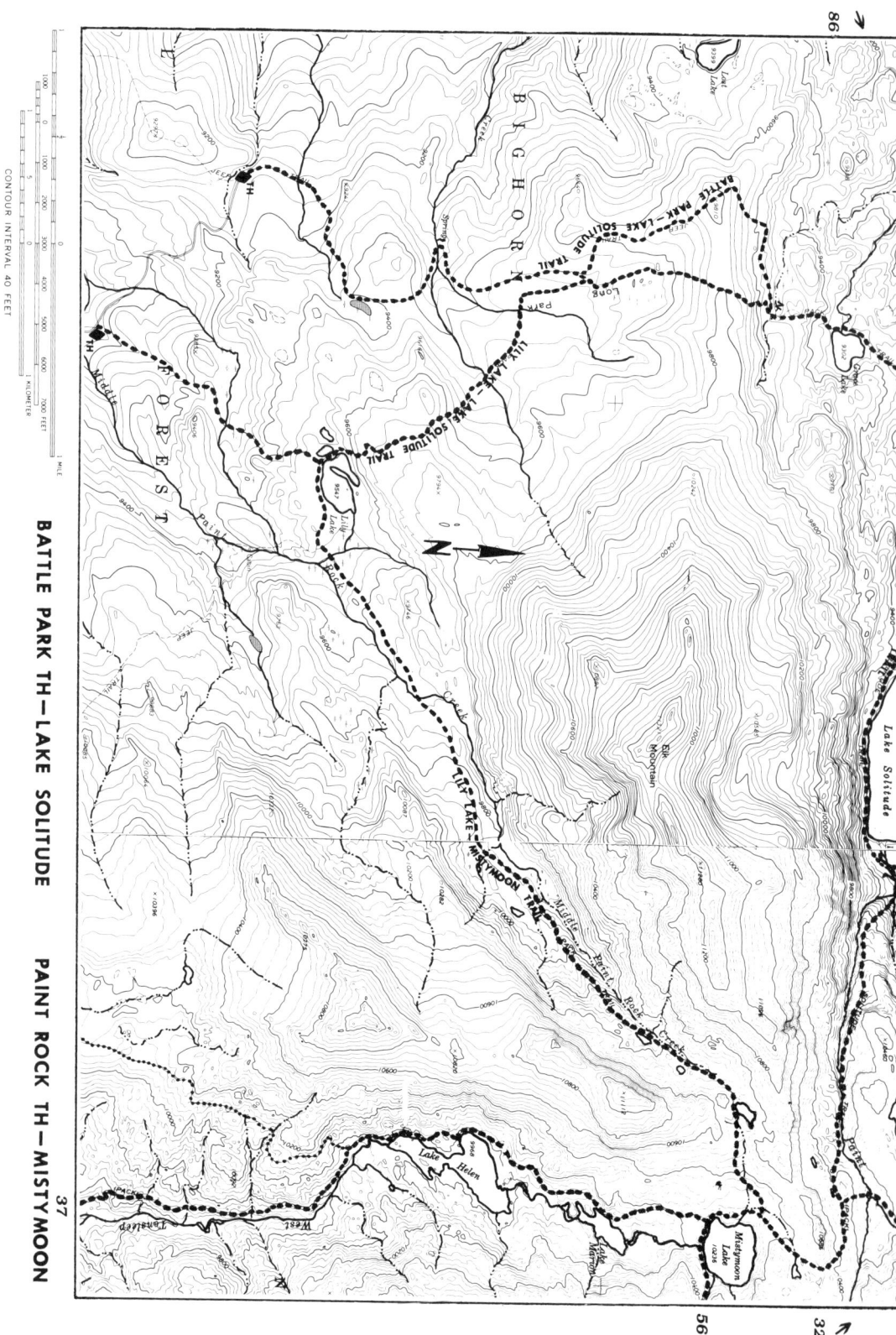

Cloud Peak
and the Wilderness Basin

The easiest approach to Cloud Peak is from the SW along Paint Rock Creek. This is referred to as the Southwest Route.

Mountain climbing equipment is not required for this 4.5 mile non-technical ascent. Do not regard this climb lightly. Under the best of conditions (warm, calm and dry), a round trip takes 6 to 7 hours - plenty of time for a sunny summer day to turn into a howling snowstorm, with Cloud Peak catching the brunt of it.

Be prepared for the worst so it may turn out for the best. Leave early in the day. Wear sturdy boots as it's rock all the way. Carry extra clothing, windbreakers, raingear, also water and high energy food. If you're unaccustomed to the altitude or the exertion, pace yourself and don't be ashamed to turn back.

The ascent begins at a small waterfall located 1.8 miles east of Lake Solitude and 0.8 mile north of Mistymoon Lake. The falls are part of the main Paint Rock stream, dropping out of the north into a lush bog etched by many sinuous channels. The Solitude Trail skirts the ridge south of this bog.

Cross the bog north to the waterfall. Climb up either side of the falls and proceed up the north side of Paint Rock Creek.

At the 0.5 mile point a smaller stream joins the main creek from the north. Follow the lesser stream and the numerous rock cairns, bearing steadily NE as you pass several small ponds.

After 2.5 miles, where you gain the broadest part of the SW ridge, look west and NW into the Wilderness Basin. Passage to this remote valley is via a drainage which runs from the SW ridge at this point.

The creek is just scattered trickles now and

Cloud Peak continually beckons as you bear more easterly towards the narrowest part of the ridge. Cross this, then turn north for the last 0.5 mile to reach the summit.

Cloud Peak, Wyoming's tenth highest point, rises 13,167' into the clouds. The peak itself is rather flat, measuring 200 yards between its east and west faces and descending gradually (700' in 0.5 mile) to the north.

In 1881 a party of six climbed Cloud Peak and left several coins in a monument of rocks. This was the first recorded ascent of the peak. Many people have since climbed the peak. In 1936, a climber reported finding thousands of frozen grasshoppers in a large snowbank under an overhang. This attests to the wind's power as it roars up the peak from the plains and valleys below.

The scene of several tragedies, the peak claimed the life of one mountain climber who fell while rappeling down one of the sheer walls. The wreckage of a small plane remains on an inaccessible ledge near the summit. One of the victims of this crash was buried on the peak in 1964.

Cloud Peak is abutted from all directions but the SW with steep ridges or walls, where several of the range's largest glaciers originated. The steepest walls are to the east and NE. These and other cirque walls in the range have been little softened by erosion since the Ice Age, and thus are as sheer as when the glaciers left them. The peak still shelters a small glacier situated at the base of the east face.

WILDERNESS BASIN

This alpine valley drains the region west of Cloud Peak and south of Black Tooth Mountain. There are two main approaches to this basin:

A. From Lake Solitude: About 0.5 mile east of the lake, where the Solitude Trail crosses Paint Rock Creek on a footbridge, the stream from the

Wilderness Basin joins the creek from the NE. Follow up this cascading stream, making your way over boulders as you bear NE and north, passing numerous rock-basin lakes along the way.

   B. From Mistymoon: Rather than descending nearly to Lake Solitude and then back up the Basin, take the Southwest Route of the Cloud Peak climb. See the Cloud Peak account for details.

The Wilderness Basin is exceptionally beautiful, but rather severe for camping: treeless, bare rock with little shelter from the elements. It is seldom visited and shows little trace of human presence, providing a rewarding trek for the conscientious and well-prepared hiker.

Wilderness Basin from SW ridge of Cloud Peak.
Photo by Marcus Johnshoy

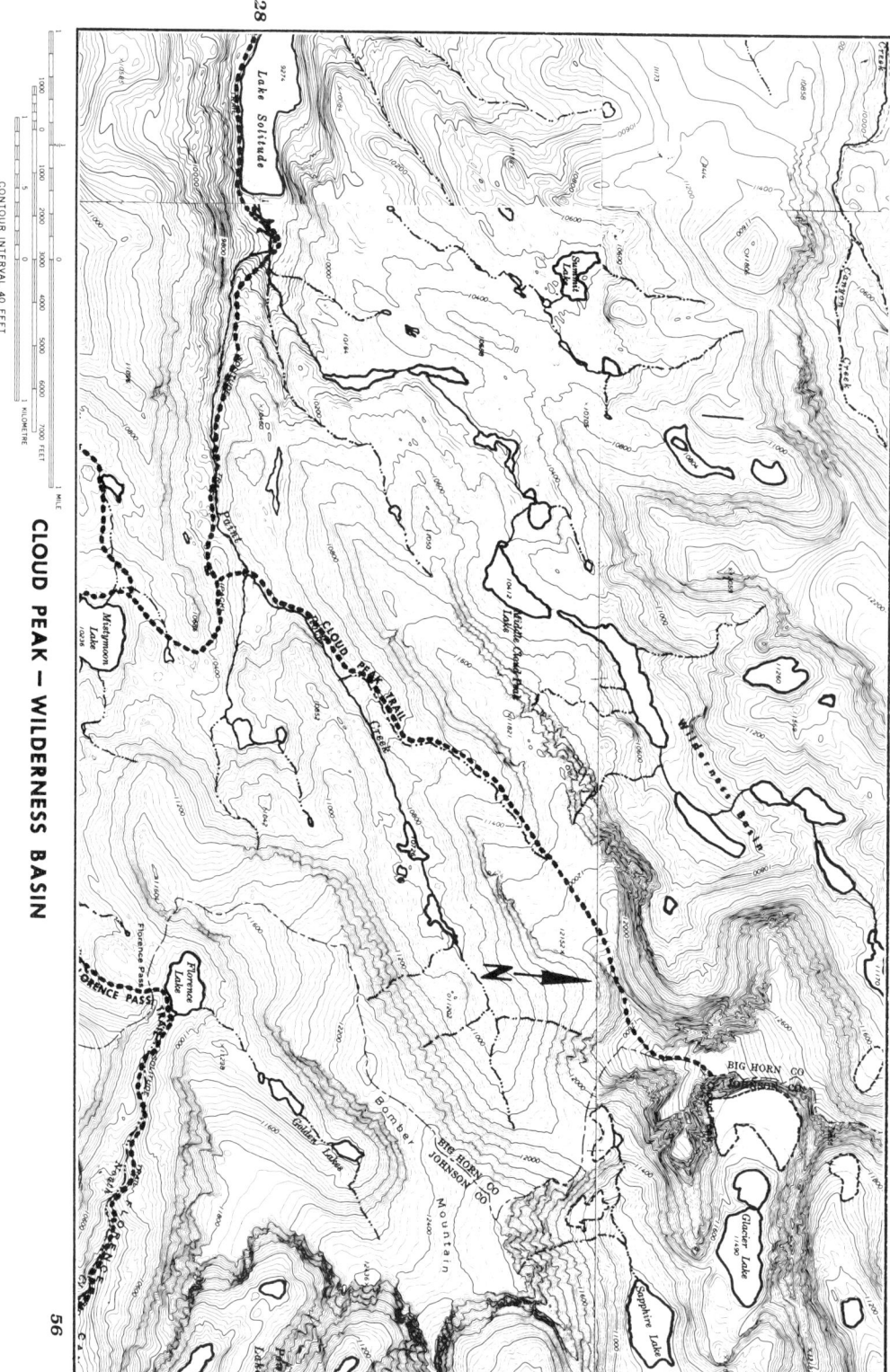

CLOUD PEAK – WILDERNESS BASIN

West Tensleep Trailhead to Mistymoon Lake

Referred to as the Mistymoon Trail, this popular trail follows West Tensleep Creek north to Lakes Helen, Marion and Mistymoon. It allows access to exquisite alpine meadows around Mistymoon, intersections with the Solitude Trail and the rugged peaks atop the Bighorn Range. It rises moderately from 9,100' to 10,250' in its 6.5 mile length.

Due to its position - in timber, low along the east side of a high lateral ridge - the trail tends to be shady and cool, with snow lingering well into July. The snow, summer rains and heavy foot and pack-animal use combine to make the trail muddy and rather toilsome at this season, especially in the 3 miles south from Lake Marion. The area from Tyrell Ranger Station to Mistymoon is also a popular cross-country skiing route in winter.

Register at the trailhead (capacity: 45 cars) located midway up the east side of West Tensleep Lake. Proceed north along the lakeshore then across meadow north of the lake. Cross West Tensleep Creek on a sturdy Forest Service bridge. About 200 yards west, across the meadow, a side trail begins at the treeline. This trail ascends steeply (800' in 1 mile) to Bald Ridge, a lateral moraine of the West Tensleep glacier, longest in the Bighorns. It then turns north with the ridge, rejoining Mistymoon Trail after 3 miles at a point 0.4 mile south of Lake Helen. Hikers gain panoramic views from Bald Ridge. Taking this trail helps relieve the overuse of the Mistymoon trail.

After the bridge, make a short steep climb into the lodgepole pine forest. Two miles of moderate-level travel later, emerge from timber at a broad wet meadow. (Near this meadow, the trail heading east is the 'Yost' Trail. This 3.5 mile 'man-way' connects with the Lost Twin Lakes Trail east of Mirror Lake. The 'Yost' Trail is a rough, hard to follow trail with no water. Travel on horseback is not possible. This trail is scheduled for gradual improvement during the next several years.) A sturdy bridge crosses a tributary of West Tensleep, but as the area is so low, the bridge is sometimes submerged in a few inches of water. It's an easy wade across but for the pools to the sides. These pools and others throughout this area are clear, calm and resplendent in moonlight or sunshine. Fishing for brook trout is excellent, but use care if you camp as campsite use is already heavy hereabouts.

Cloud Peak as seen from atop Bald Ridge.
Photo by JoAnn Emerson

The next 2 miles to Lake Helen are moderate-level, passing through shady timber on a trail often muddy and/or snowy-slushy. Trail emerges on the south shore of Lake Helen in its rocky basin. Careful scrutiny of the rock reveals striations

Skiing, Bald Ridge. *Photo by JoAnn Emerson.*

generally oriented downstream, gouged by glacier-borne boulders.

The area around and above Lake Helen receives a great deal of camping and fishing pressure. Here the flora is subalpine - fir and spruce - which grows shorter and less extensively than the flora downstream where the climate is milder and soil is deeper.

As you pass west of Lake Helen, look for Cloud Peak, highest in the Bighorns (13,167'), on the northern horizon.

Three-fourths mile of moderate hiking through rocky meadows brings you to Lake Marion, expressing the shape of its basin with its irregular outline. As at Helen, wood is scarce and becoming more scarce from increasing use; a gas stove is necessary for cooking.

From Marion climb north towards Mistymoon Lake, gaining impressive views of West Tensleep valley. At Mistymoon the climate is alpine; fires are prohibited and a stove is necessary for cooking.

Trails intersecting near Mistymoon lead to Florence Pass and North Clear to the east (p. 50); Middle Paint Rock Creek and Lily Lake to the SW (p. 26); and Lake Solitude (p. 22) and points north including Cloud Peak (p. 29).

Mistymoon Lake with Cloud Peak on horizon, center.
Photo by U.S. Forest Service

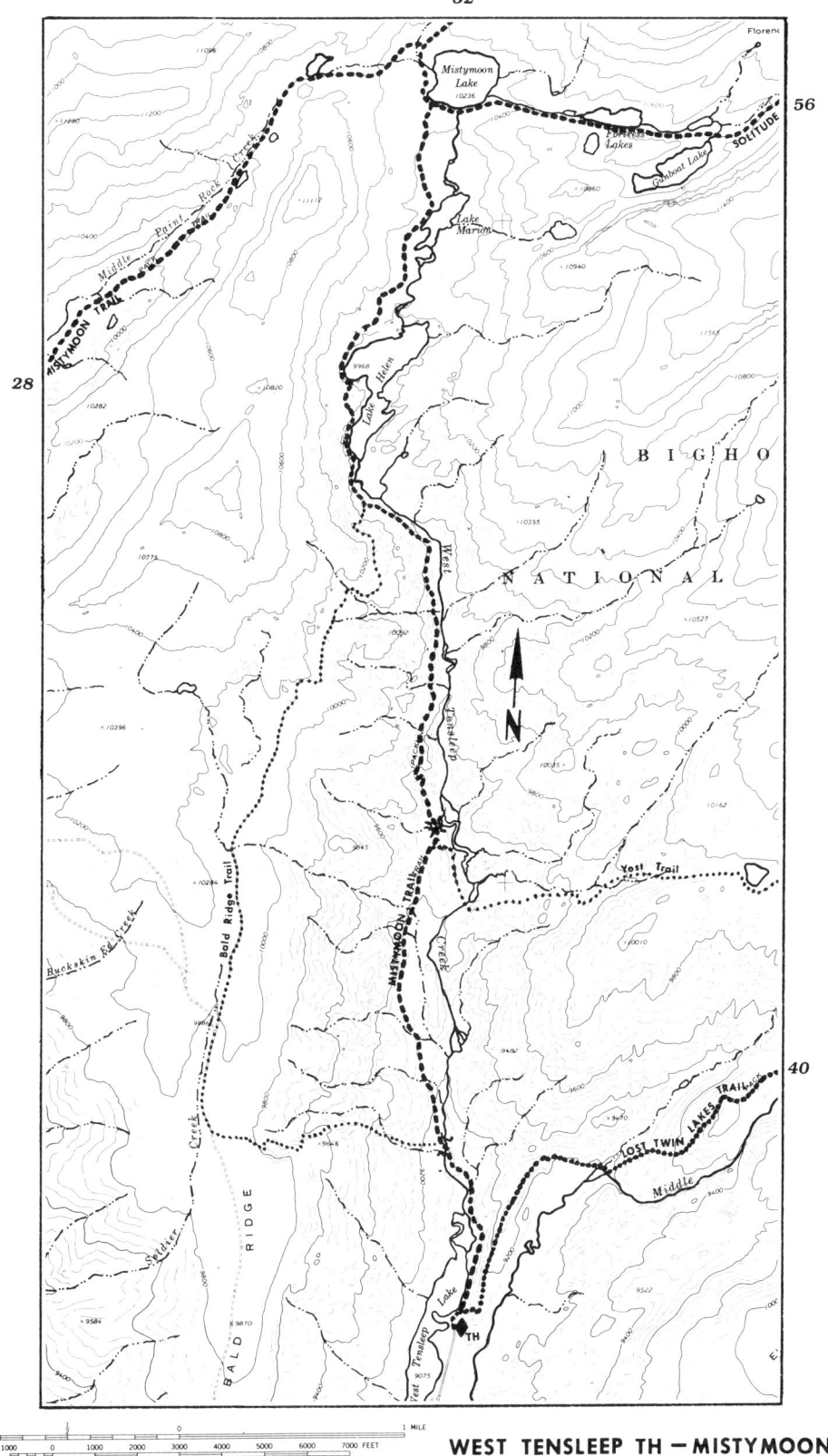

WEST TENSLEEP TH – MISTYMOON

West Tensleep Trailhead to Lost Twin Lakes

This trail leads through deep forest and grassy meadows along Middle Tensleep Creek, terminating at its head in the glacier-scooped cirques holding Lost Twin Lakes beneath sheer cliffs up to 1,600' high. The trail is moderate with some steep passages, gaining 1,200' in elevation over its 6.5 mile length. Good water is found just NE of Lost Twin Lakes.

From the trailhead on the east shore of West Tensleep Lake, follow the Lost Twins Trail NE through mature forest, up and over a low ridge. The trail levels off and turns east then descends for a brief visit with Middle Tensleep Creek and its meadow skirt. Re-enter the woods, heading NE for 1.5 miles, over another ridge to a tributary of Middle Tensleep.

Register and enter the wilderness 2.5 miles from the trailhead. (Forest Service plans to move the registration box to trailhead.) Cross the tributary on rocks 0.5 mile farther on, and turn south through meadow. Mirror Lake is a short walk east from the trail. This pristine lake is on the tributary which drains the country south of Mather Peaks.

From here the trail is level-moderate, paralleling Middle Tensleep on its sunny, dry north side. After 2 miles, two forks merge their waters into one stream, Middle Tensleep Creek. The stream from the SE flows from Lost Twin Lakes 1.5 miles away; the other fork descends from the NE and the pass (11,300') west of Lake Angeline, 2.5 miles away.

The latter (north) fork may be followed all the way to the pass and over to Lake Angeline, leading to the region east and north of Angeline. It's a steady, moderate-steep climb to the alpine pass, earning views of the horizons east and west. The descent is slow, laborious clambering over boulders on the ridge north of Lake Angeline. This is an unsanctioned, unmarked route suggested for experienced and properly equipped hikers. Horseback access on this route is impossible.

To reach Lost Twin Lakes, cross the north fork (rocks or logs) and head SE up a moderate-steep ridge in subalpine timber. Where the trail emerges at the south fork, the lower lake may be reached by crossing the creek and hiking up the rock face which drops in terraces from the south - not difficult but slippery and precarious if wet with snow or ice. Otherwise, the trail follows drainage at the base of the ridge to the east, emerging from timber at the north side of the lower lake.

The Lost Twin Lakes are clear and cold, rock-rimmed and overshadowed by awesome cliffs. These glacier-scored walls are among the highest in the Bighorns.

Campsites are along the north edge of the lower lake, but this sublime subalpine area should be respected by visiting only; camp lower down where the impact is less damaging.

Cliffs above Lost Twin Lakes.
Photo by M. Melius

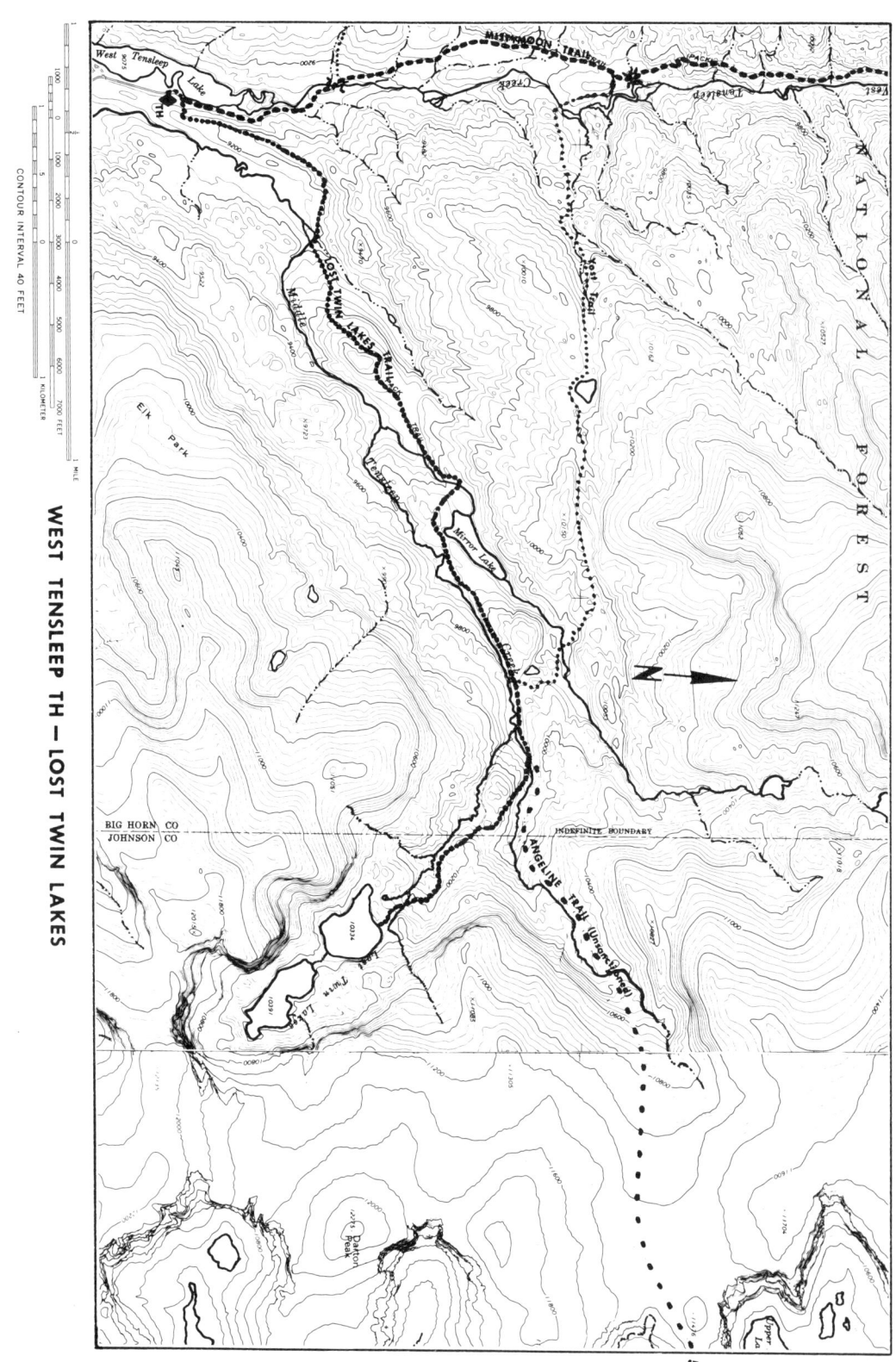

WEST TENSLEEP TH – LOST TWIN LAKES

Circle Park Trailhead to Sherd Lake Loop

This trail allows access to the SE corner of the Primitive Area, a region remarkable for its classic glacial topography and its history of fire and subsequent recovery. The Sherd Lake Loop is about 11 miles in length.

Throughout this area look for signs of the Duck Creek fire of August, 1943: the charred remains of burnt spruce and pine, some standing, most fallen; thickets of spindly lodgepole pine, the first to recover after a fire (its cones open in the heat, scattering the seeds for the new forest). In some places, near Long Lake, for instance, the fire was so hot that it sterilized what little soil there is in this rocky country, recovery has been meager, and the scene is still one of stark devastation: skeletal trees standing amidst logs strewn like toothpicks (roughly aligned with the prevailing NW winds).

The fire was started by lightning and consumed nearly 10,000 acres (15 square miles) before being brought under control after 18 days. Some 820 men fought the blaze. Two months later the first heavy snowfall quenched the still-smoldering, smoking region.

Register at the west end of Circle Park campground. From here the trail begins a moderate ascent of the terminal moraine of the South Clear Creek Glacier, the largest and steepest moraine in the Bighorns. The rise to the ridge of this moraine is some 400' in 1 mile.

After gaining the ridge, the trail enters the level ground moraine, composed of drift material (boulders) deposited behind the terminal moraine. This area is pockmarked with numerous ponds, some of which are skirted by the trail as it approaches Sherd Lake from the NE. At the east end of the lake the trail forks, south to the South Fork Ponds area and north across the creek to junction with the Long Lake Trail, (side trail A). At this junction the trail turns west towards Rainy Lake. The first 0.5 mile is moderate but the last mile is moderate-steep, a gain of 600' in 1.5 miles. Just east of Rainy Lake is the junction to Willow Lake, (side trail B). The trail turns south at Rainy continuing moderate-steep for a mile to the Old Crow junction, (side trail C). From there the trail is moderate-level as it heads SE, crossing South Clear Creek on rocks just east of Her Lake. Trail is moderate as it descends east, passing just north of Trigger Lake and crossing Duck Creek at its outlet. From there the trail descends with Duck Creek, turning NE and recrossing the creek before a moderate ascent into the marshy South Fork Ponds area. The trail levels off with the terrain and crosses South Clear Creek just east of a pond. From there it's less than a mile NW to the junction at Sherd Lake.

SIDE TRAILS

A. LONG LAKE: This moderate trail heads west from the junction north of Sherd Lake, passing through barren, rocky terrain for 1 mile to Long Lake. The scene here is one of burnt desolation, but the new growth rising amidst it is a joy to behold. The water drains from Ringbone Lake into the north side of Long Lake, roaring as it falls through the boulders there.

B. WILLOW LAKE: From the junction east of Rainy Lake, a moderate trail heads NW for 1.4 miles along the ridge south of Oliver Creek to Willow Lake, another boulder-rimmed lake like all those in this valley. From here it is possible to boulder-hop upstream to the deep cirque NE of Darton Peak, but as with any off-trail travel in this region, it's very rugged going.

From Otter Lake it is possible to follow the

drainage up to Darton Peak - again rugged, slow going over jagged boulders and criss-crossed logs. At Darton you have access to Bighorn Peak and a view to the west - Lost Twin Lakes and Middle Tensleep valley. Such a trip (from Otter Lake) would take a full summer's day for the strongest hiker and is not recommended for the novice or casual hiker.

C. OLD CROW: Lake is 0.5 mile from the junction. From there you have access to Lame Deer Lake and the Chill Lakes. What trail there is, is hard to make out, so make your own way on boulders and logs, following the creek up the narrow valley. The cirques east and north of Bighorn Peak are some of the deepest in the Bighorns, up to 1,200' high.

Rainy Lake area, Bighorn Peak on left, Darton Peak on right. *Photo by M. Melius*

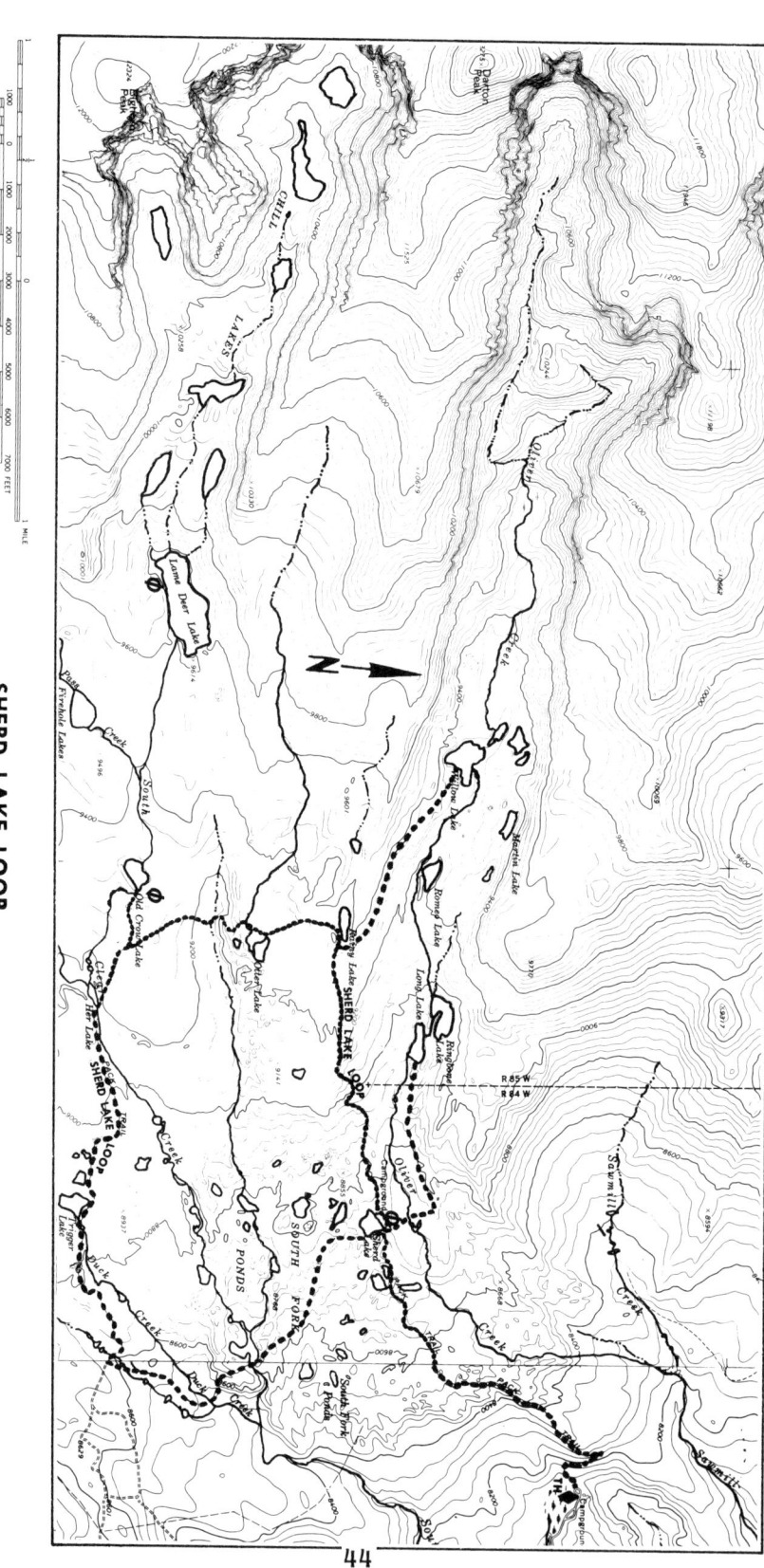

Hunter Corrals Trailhead to Seven Brothers Lakes

This is a 7 mile hike with an elevation gain of 1,900' east to west. The first 3 miles are through the open, rolling hills of Hunter Mesa and Buffalo Park. The last 4 miles are moderate-steep through lodgepole pine, spruce and fir. The popular Seven Brothers Lakes are renowned for their scenery; this popularity causes frequent overuse of the area and heavy fishing pressure. From the lakes, hikers can climb 3 miles to the steep-walled cirque holding Lake Angeline - a rewarding day hike.

Leave the west end of Hunter Corrals Trailhead, cross Hunter Creek and climb trail on left, south up the hill. (Trail right, going west, leads to Soldier Park and Mistymoon, this trail has a steep, 1 mile connecting trail to Seven Brothers Lakes.) Continue south on a narrow road, pass through a gate and zigzag down to North Clear Creek; good campsites on the east bank of North Clear Creek (closed to vehicles beyond this point). Look for deer in this area at dusk and dawn; listen for coyotes at night. Cross North Clear Creek on a log footbridge, (the confluence of North Clear Creek and Seven Brothers Creek is 400 yards south of this crossing) and enter east end of Buffalo Park.

The walk through Buffalo Park is level. A small, flowing spring is just south of the trail at the west end of Buffalo Park. From the west end of the park, Seven Brothers Lakes are 4 miles west through timber. Wind upward NW through stands of slender lodgepole pine; 1 mile from Buffalo Park, the trail bends SW. Trail is moderate-steep. Built over rocks, the trail is well-marked and easy to follow. This area is the terminal moraine of four mile long Lake Creek Glacier.

Three miles west of Buffalo Park, pass junction with trail heading north down the ridge to Trail

Park. Continue on trail heading west towards Seven Brothers. After 0.5 mile, pass the north shore of the first lake of the Seven Brothers chain.

Trail bends SW and is level past the second lake. A dim trail heading SE between the second and third lakes leads to Lake Angeline (p. 48).

Seven Brothers Lakes area. *Photo by Marcus Johnshoy*

The trail stays on top of the ridge and passes between lakes three and four. A large, flat camping area and wilderness guard station are located between the third and fourth lakes. Trail descends west past lakes five and six. The trail ends on the east shore of the seventh lake. Camping available just north of trail's end. The east shore of the seventh lake is sandy and suitable for wading, (use caution, water is very cold).

The Seven Brothers chain is in a basin carved out by the Lake Creek Glacier. Some of the lakes of the chain were formed by the deposition of glacial drift, the other lakes are rock basins. The shorelines of all the lakes are heaped with boulders.

Hikers can walk and boulder-hop up the valley west of the seventh lake to the large cirque holding Upper and Lower Frozen Lakes. This is a difficult hike with no trail. The high cliffs that shade the Frozen Lakes are quite visible from the Seven Brothers area.

To gain a spectacular view of the North Clear Creek Valley and Florence Canyon to the west, climb the grass covered ridge north of the fourth, fifth and sixth lakes. The easiest way up this ridge is to follow the west shore of the fourth lake through the timber then switchback up the south slope of the ridge.

Seven Brothers Lakes to Lake Angeline

This connecting trail covers over 3 miles with an elevation gain of 700'. The trail is moderate-steep, especially in the last mile to Lake Angeline. An altitude above 10,000' makes this last mile strenuous: proceed slowly. This trail is a good hike for those camped at Seven Brothers. The Lake Angeline area offers an example of a small, half-moon cirque with a snowfield at its base. Tremendous views in all directions reward those who boulder-hop the ridge NW of Angeline.

Begin the hike just north of the crossing between the second and third lakes of the Seven Brothers chain. Trail origin is difficult to find especially if the signs have been stolen. From the main Seven Brothers trail, head SE stepping on rocks to cross three small streams near the east shore of third lake. Cross the land bridge separating lakes two and three and enter the heavy timber just south of the lakes.

Climb moderately for 2 miles through lodgepole pine and rock fields, then come upon a junction with an east-west trail. Trail west leads to Angeline. (The trail heading east from this junction descends to Webber Park 2 miles east. From Webber Park the trail (a jeep trail) crosses Schoolhouse Park for 2 miles to Hwy. 16. There is no trailhead at Webber or Schoolhouse Park. The Forest Service advises against parking in these areas because they are not patrolled. Hikers are also discouraged from driving to and parking in this area because these park roads are subject to seasonal road closures.)

One-half mile west of this junction, the timber ends; Lake Angeline is 0.7 of a mile west over barren, rocky slopes. Above timberline, the trail is well-marked with rock cairns.

Lake Angeline lies in a crescent cirque which

didn't create a glacier of any appreciable size. A perpetual snowfield exists just west of Lake Angeline at the base of the west wall. Those who climb the boulder-strewn ridge just north and west of Lake Angeline will gain a panoramic view of the Seven Brothers basin and the plains to the east. Continue to climb west of this ridge to peak "11,476" for a magnificent view of the west slope of the Bighorns and the Bighorn Basin beyond.

Lake Angeline cirque. *Photo by Ken Melius*

Hunter Corrals Trailhead to Mistymoon Lake

This popular trail follows North Clear Creek through dense woods and open parks; through Florence Canyon, deep and serene; and up and over Florence Pass on the granite mantle of the Bighorn Range. It provides connections with two trails going north to Elk Lake and with one south to Seven Brothers Lakes. The trail is moderate with some steep passages while rising 3,000' in 14.5 miles. There are numerous fishing and camping opportunities along the way.

The trail originates at Hunter Corrals, (capacity: 30 cars; horse corrals). Register at the west end of the corrals, cross Hunter Creek and head up the hill, taking the trail to the right. (Trail left leads south to Buffalo Park and Seven Brothers Lakes (p. 45). The right trail goes west on a jeep trail through open terrain, then enters timber and ascends moderately with some steep passages for the next 2 miles. After 1 mile, cross a gauging station for North Clear Creek and continue NW. You are now in the broad expanse of the terminal moraine of North Clear Creek Glacier. This area is characterized by many small lakes and ridges created during the retreat of the glacier.

The trail is still a well-worn, rocky jeep trail as it bends west to enter the eastern extension of Soldier Park. Here lie the graves of Peter Garde and Carl Johnson. In the 1890's a grave marked with a cross was found at this site. It was assumed that a soldier was buried here so the large park was named Soldier Park. However, the late August Hettinger, a Forest Ranger, determined through research that Garde was a French civil engineer working with an army survey party in 1877. He was accidentally shot while cleaning his rifle. Ranger Hettinger constructed the log enclosure for the grave. Johnson, a Swedish sawmill employee, died of a heart attack here in 1922.

Just west of these graves, enter the grassy expanse of Soldier Park. The trail soon splits. (Trail north leads to Elk Lake via Triangle Park (p. 57). Steer west through Soldier Park. Many fine camping spots are in this area.

Soldier Park is an example of a shallow lake being filled by glacial debris. Before this valley's glacier retreated, the park was probably a shallow lake located on the terminal moraine. As the glacier melted and regressed, boulders, gravel, and sediment carried downstream and filled the lake. The glacier's 600' high south lateral moraine begins at Soldier Park and extends west for several miles.

The trail re-enters timber, lodgepole pine and Engelmann spruce, at the west end of the park and continues west. Spruce and subalpine fir become more prominent from the 9,000' level to timberline.

Leave the timber 1.5 miles west of Soldier Park, and enter a small clearing at the edge of North Clear Creek. This marks the end of motorized travel, an area also overcamped. From here the fairly level foot and horse trail continues west through clearings and timber.

One mile further enter the long, narrow Trail Park. Here a fork leads south to Seven Brothers Lakes. It's a steep, 1 mile hike to the lowest of the seven lakes. (Forest Service bridge across North Clear Creek marks the beginning of this trail.)

Continue on the main trail west through Trail Park, then north into timber. Come upon a junction with a trail going north to Elk Lake (p. 57). Two miles west of Trail Park, cross to the south side of the creek on a sturdy Forest Service bridge. Camping is available just before this crossing, with several small streams (good water) coming off the ridge to the north. Deer Lake is 0.4 mile NE of the crossing.

The section of trail west of the crossing might be muddy with some snow lingering in June and July. After a mile, recross to the north side. A log foot bridge at the crossing may be washed out. If so, use care in wading the cold creek with its strong current. Florence Pass is about 3.5 miles west of the crossing.

View from Trail Park, west to Florence Canyon.
Photo by Pete Carrels

A short hike brings you to Medicine Cabin Park, in the deep and narrow Florence Canyon. North Clear Creek skirts the wall to the south. Powell Creek, coming from the north, is crossed on rocks or a log bridge. (A steep hike up the rugged creekbed brings you to Powell Lakes, in cirques protected by 1,000' walls.)

The wet subalpine meadow of Medicine Cabin Park, with water tumbling down the granite walls to the south, is one of the most splendid areas of the Bighorns. At the west end of the park, begin a steep, zigzag ascent along the north side of Florence

Waterslide on south wall of Florence Canyon.
Photo by Marcus Johnshoy

Canyon. Pace yourself, remembering that you are rising above 10,000'. From here to Mistymoon snow persists for most of the year.

The talus rubble at the base of the canyon walls is an example of frost erosion - frost expanding and shattering the rock into ever-greater disorder.

One and one-half miles from Medicine Cabin Park, (12.5 miles from Hunter Corrals) reach the icy rock basin holding Florence Lake. About thirty yards SE of the lake's outlet, look for a bronze plaque.

Located on the ground, the plaque is a memorial listing the names of ten army airmen who died on June 28, 1943. They were aboard a B-17 which crashed into the SW ridge of a 12,840' summit 1.5 miles north of Florence Lake. The summit was named Bomber Mountain in 1946 by the Sheridan chapter of the American War Dads, who dedicated the memorial. The wreckage was on the remote mountain for two years before it was discovered by two cowboys who saw sunlight reflecting from weathered metal.

From Florence Lake turn south and climb up over Florence Pass. This marks the west end of the North Clear Creek Glacier and the beginning of the West Tensleep Glacier. As the trail is snow-covered much of the year, it may be easier to walk on boulders where possible. The trail curves SW with the valley, passing north of Gunboat Lake and south of the larger of the Fortress Lakes. From here it's a 0.5 mile scramble down the rugged, rocky drainage to the beautiful Mistymoon Lake. Here and in all alpine areas above timberline no fires are permitted; bring a gas stove for cooking if you camp this high.

Trails intersecting at Mistymoon lead south to West Tensleep Lake (p. 33), SW to Lily Lake (p. 26), and NW to Lake Solitude (p. 22), and the easiest route to Cloud Peak (p. 29).

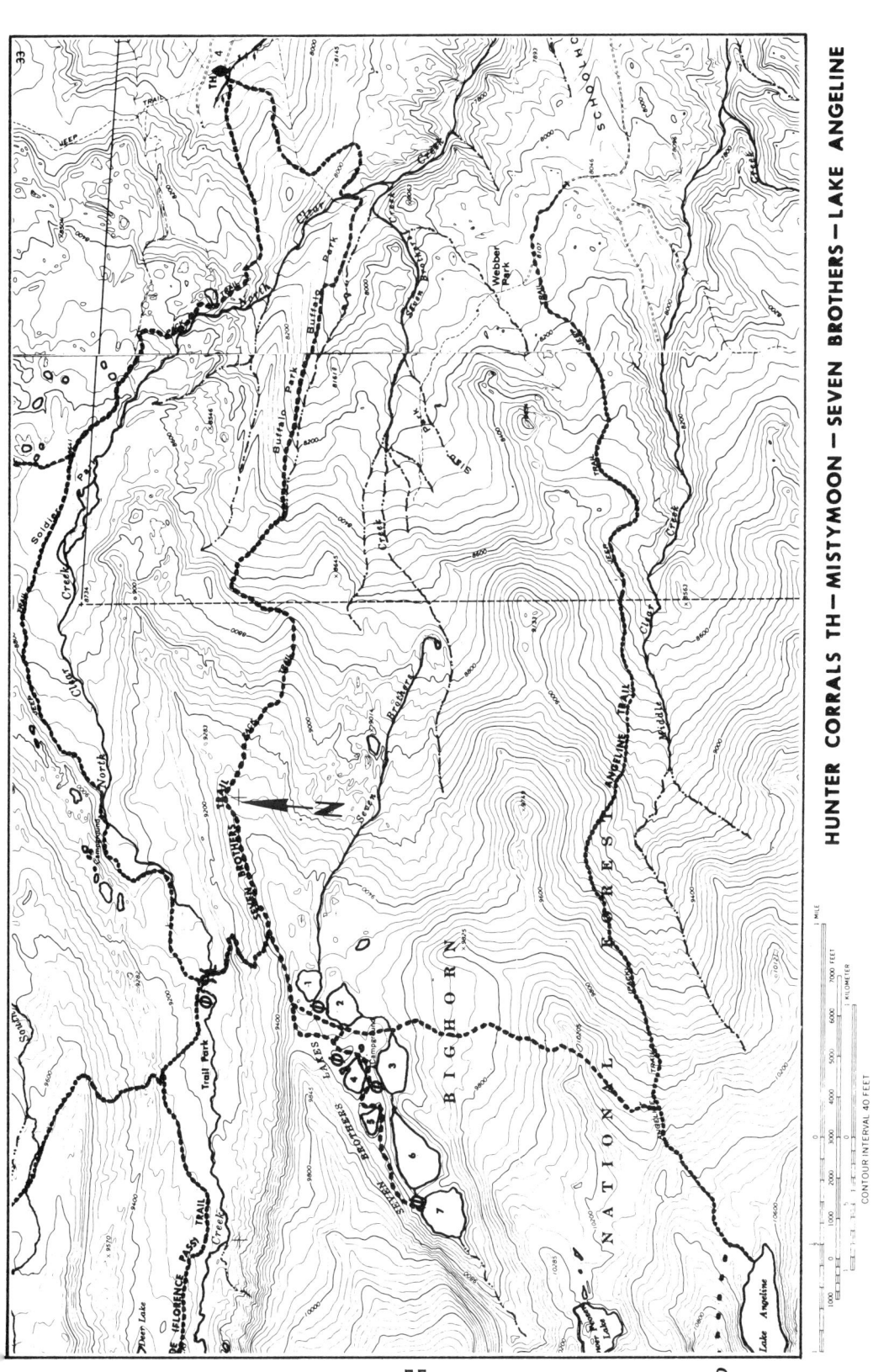

HUNTER CORRALS TH — MISTYMOON — SEVEN BROTHERS — LAKE ANGELINE

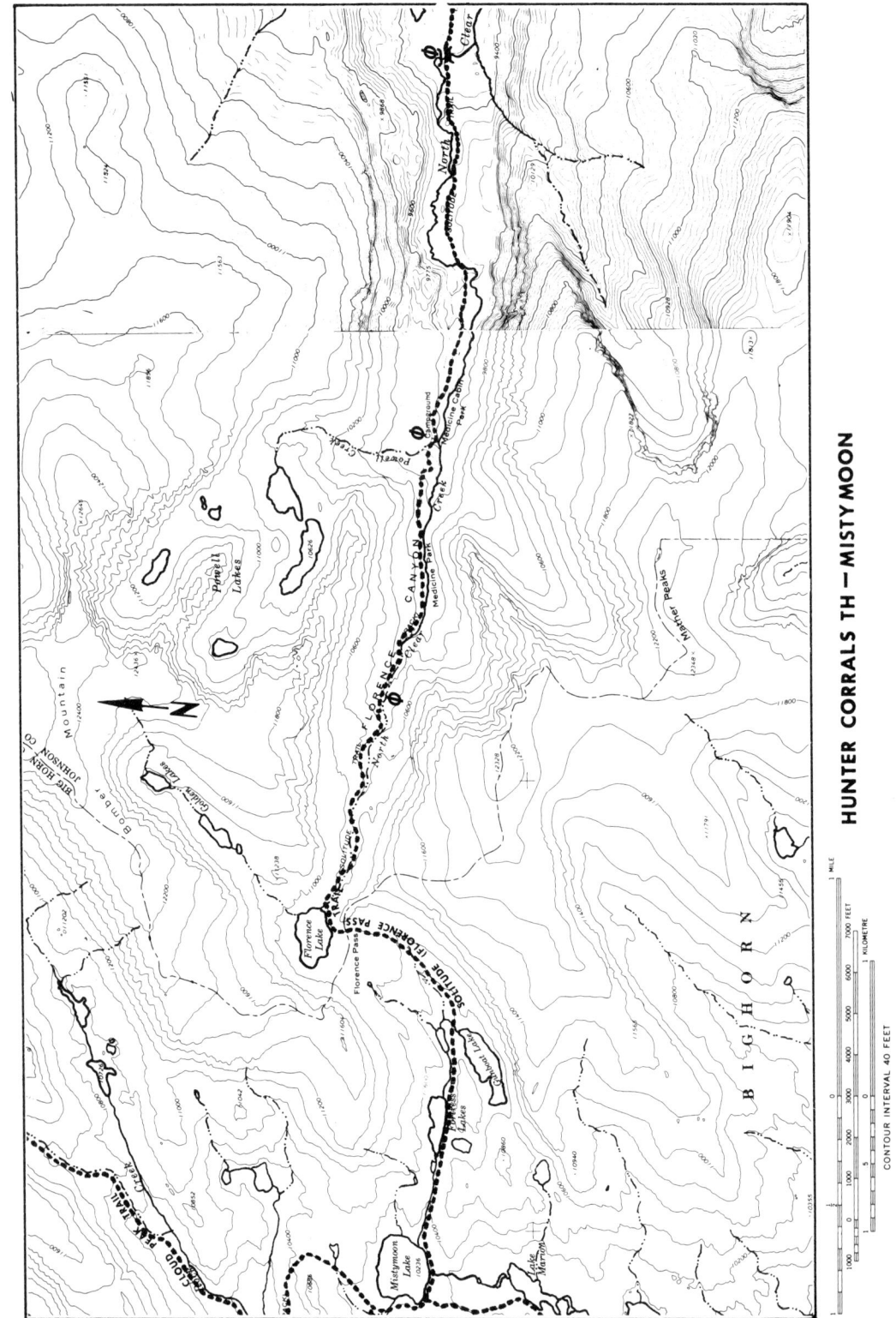

HUNTER CORRALS TH – MISTY MOON

Color Plates

A - A source, ultimately to a river. Middle Tensleep valley. By M. Melius.

B - Winter, near Lake Marion. By Randy Brich.

C - North Clear Creek valley, Florence Canyon on left. By Ken Melius.

D - Cliff Lake. By Marcus Johnshoy.

E - Autumn, North Clear Creek near Soldier Park. By Ken Melius.

F - Lake Solitude. By U.S. Forest Service

G - Waterslide, Wilderness Basin. By Randy Brich.

H - Bighorn Peak. Lame Deer Lake in foreground. By JoAnn Emerson.

I - Cloud Peak, left of center. Elk Lake, right. By M. Melius.

J - Spear Lake. Exit Pass, above, right of center. By JoAnn Emerson.

K - Early morning, from above Buffalo Park. Darton Peak, left. by Ken Melius.

L - Highland Park and beyond. Left to right, Penrose Peak, Sawtooth Ridge, Mt. Woolsey and Black Tooth. By M. Melius.

M - Jagged wall between Black Tooth and Cloud Peak. By Randy Brich.

N - Black Tooth at sunset. By JoAnn Emerson.

O - Glacier and Diamond Lakes, from atop Cloud Peak. By JoAnn Emerson.

P - Indian Paintbrush, Highland Lake. By JoAnn Emerson.

Q - Alpine Forget-me-not. By M. Melius.

R - Autumn, near Lake Golden. By M. Melius.

S - Lake Elsa. By Marcus Johnshoy.

<u>Front Cover:</u> Spear Lake. By JoAnn Emerson.

<u>Back Cover:</u> Parry Primrose. By JoAnn Emerson.

A

D

E

F

H

I

K

L

O

P

Q

R

Elk Lake Loop

This account describes a loop from Soldier Park to Elk Lake and back with no backtracking; a good two day hike.

This trail leads through the remote and little-used country of the South and Middle Rock Creeks to the high, expansive valley containing Elk Lake. From here one sees and may approach the great walls enclosing cirques east and NE of Cloud Peak. By Elk Lake the trail joins the Solitude Trail north to Willow Park Reservoir and Highland Park Trails. The trail is moderate with steep passages, gaining 1,500' over its 6 mile length. Good water is first found 4 miles from Soldier Park.

From the junction at the east edge of Soldier Park, follow the moderate-steep trail north 0.7 mile to Triangle Park, a lush meadow with the aptly named Ant Hill to the NW. Turn west along south edge of park, then north across South Rock Creek on a foot bridge. The trail is level for 0.5 mile through the park, then climbs moderate-steep 1.5 miles to a NE-facing ridge. Numerous rock outcroppings dot this landscape, with views of the heavily-forested Rock Creeks east and NE, and the Ant Hill to the west.

Another 1.5 miles of moderate-steep trail brings you to the ridge, 10,200', east of Elk Lake. (Look for good water in small streams running north from Ant Hill.) This ridge allows the best views of the Cloud Peak - Penrose Peak region. From there it's 1.5 miles NW to Elk Lake.

Near the ridgetop (on the west slope) the trail forks to Gem Lake, about 1.5 miles north (moderate). One-half mile before reaching Gem Lake, this trail forks west to Cloud Peak Reservoir (and beyond that: Mead Lake and the spectacular cirques east of Cloud Peak), crossing Solitude Trail after 0.5 mile. This provides a short cut to the Solitude Trail north, instead of going past Elk Lake.

The main trail goes through great boulder fields before crossing Elk Creek (rocks or shaky logs) just north of the lake. The creek appears to flow uphill north from here. This lake was formed when the Mead Glacier which gouged out South Piney Creek dammed Elk Creek downstream. When the glacier receded, its lateral moraine was left as a dam.

Trail joins Solitude Trail just west of Elk Lake. (Trail north leads to Willow Park and Highland Park Trails, p. 67). Head south from junction and ascend 1.5 miles to the pass west of the Ant Hill. There is good water in many rivulets coursing down this alpine bowl to Elk Lake. At the pass, good views may be had of Elk Lake to the north and North Clear Creek to the south, but Cloud Peak is obscured by intervening ridges.

From the pass descend on this drier, south side for 1.5 miles, moderate-steep. Then, 1 mile of moderate trail crosses South Rock Creek and a bald ridge (the north lateral moraine of North Clear Creek Glacier) to the south before descending steeply for 0.5 mile to junction with the Soldier Park Trail. (Trail west leads to Florence Pass, p. 51). From here it's 3 miles of moderate-level trail east to Soldier Park, completing the loop.

ELK LAKE LOOP — SOUTHERN SECTION

View east, towards Ant Hill. *Photo by M. Melius*

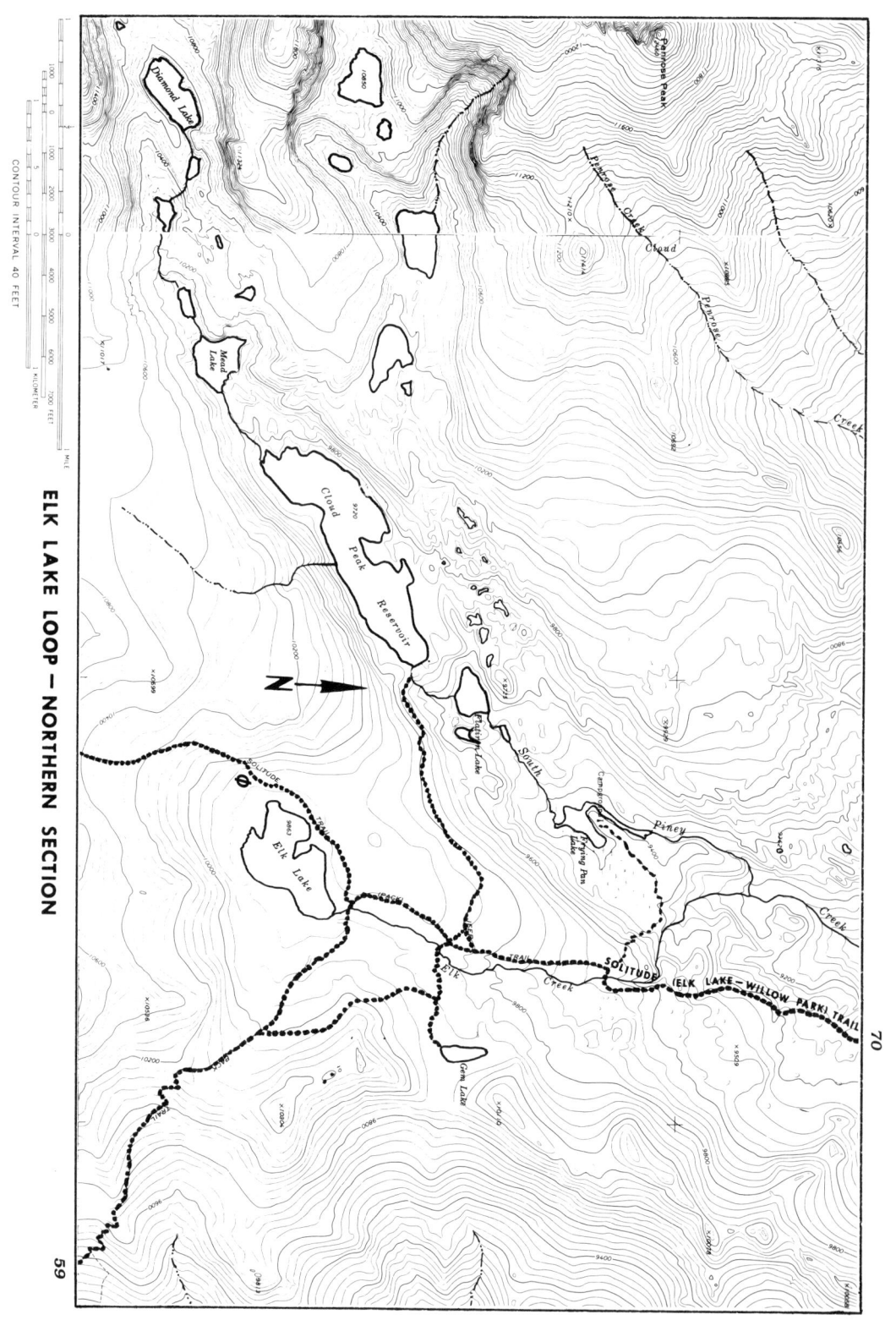

Cross Creek Trailhead to Highland Park, Spear Lake and Elk Lake

The Highland Park area offers impressive views of Penrose Peak, the Sawtooth Ridge, Hallelujah Peak and others - the jagged NE wall of the range. The Highland lakes are nestled in their basins south of the park; Spear Lake, wedged into its narrow canyon, is SW of the park. Kearny Lake Reservoir, Willow Park Reservoir and the trail to Elk Lake are all in heavy timber SE of Highland Park. This account describes a network of trails from Cross Creek Trailhead to Highland Park where the trails split and lead SW to Spear Lake and SE to Elk Lake.

Cross Creek Trailhead to Highland Park covers 9 miles with an elevation gain of 2,000'. Good water should be available just north of the park at the East Fork of Little Goose Creek. Elk Lake is 14 miles SE of Highland Park. These 13 miles include a gradual descent of 1,600' to Willow Park Reservoir then an ascent of 1,200' in the 5 miles from Willow Park south to Elk Lake. Good water should be found south of Elk Lake.

Two routes originate at the Cross Creek Trailhead. The rough road heading SW from the trailhead leads to Coffeen Park 2 miles south. The hiking trail south from Coffeen Park joins trails to Lake Geneva, south; Edelman Pass, SW and Cross Creek Reservoir, east.

The other trail, the shortest route from the trailhead to Highland Park, passes Bighorn Reservoir. From the trailhead, walk north, up the road a short distance until reaching a fork, (fork is just south of Spear-O-Wigwam Resort). Take the road SE, to Bighorn Reservoir. The road passes the west shore of the reservoir and heads south, joining an east-west trail. This junction is midway between Bighorn and Cross Creek reservoirs. At this junction (trail west is a new, 2.5 mile, moderate-steep route to East Fork of Big Goose Creek and a junction with trails south to Lake Geneva, SW to Edelman Pass and north to Coffeen Park). Turn east and go over Cross Creek on a wooden footbridge.

The trail is moderate-steep for the next 2.5 miles, heading east then SE to a flat ridge at 9,800'. Here the trail is marked with rock cairns in terrain dominated by short (3'-20'), young spruce and pine. Good views may be had to the north (Bighorn Reservoir) and S-SW (Cross Creek valley and cliffs around the cirque lakes at its head).

From here the trail bears S-SE for 2.5 miles of moderate-level walking. At timberline look west into the Cross Creek drainage and north to the Little Goose Creeks. (At 2 miles a trail from the East Fork Little Goose Creek joins in from the NE.) Ascend the ridge east to the reaches of the East Fork of Little Goose Creek. The trail winds down moderately to the SE, crossing the creek after 1 mile. This high creek with its lush flora provides good drinking water.

From the water, ascend NE over saddle (10,400') to Highland Park. This large alpine meadow approaches the ethereal, with the great peaks of the Bighorn divide piercing even thinner air to the south. Walk into the park for a better view of these peaks so esteemed by climbers. From east to west they are: Penrose Peak and the Sawtooth Ridge extending SW; Hallelujah, sharp and narrow with the Buffalo Back sloping north in front; Black Tooth Mountain (13,005') with its deep canyon and the Five Fingers peaks to the west.

From this point it appears that these peaks rise almost directly from the southern edge of the park. But there's a mile-wide, 600' - deep valley between. The glacier which filled this valley carved into the plateau of the park, leaving it with a steep ridge to the south and east. This glacier also left three 'hanging valleys' - Penrose, Black Tooth and Five Fingers to the south. This results from the main (Kearny Creek) ice sheet having been thicker than the ice flows in the tributaries. Its greater mass cut deeper, and left the other valleys some 300'-500' above.

Penrose Canyon with Black Tooth on right, Mt. Woolsey in center (sharp spire). *Photo by U.S. Forest Service*

Although Highland Park itself was untouched by the glacier, it was the site of huge snowdrifts blown over from the west and settling in the lee. At most there was a slow creeping movement of the snow southward, while the boulders beneath were wedged apart by the alternate freezing and thawing of water. Also, rocks from ridges above rolled onto the snow and settled in. Today this 'felsenmeer' or 'sea of rock' (also evident around Elk Lake) supports dwarf grasses and forbs in the brief periods between snows.

From the NW corner of the park a choice of routes must be made: either SE across the park and then east to Kearny Lake Reservoir and beyond to Willow Park Reservoir; or south along the west edge of the park to Highland Lake and Spear Lake. The trail on the west will be officially abandoned as will the trail beyond the east edge of the park, once the Forest Service establishes a trail running SW from the east edge to link the park with the Spear Lake trail (see map). Reasons given for this change are: the trail on the west is very steep south of the park, and the east trail (past Lake Winnie) goes through bogs and is often muddy.

The trails across Highland Park are dim but marked with cairns and posts. The trail on the west side heads S-SW for a mile to the edge of the park, then descends steeply on switchbacks for 0.7 of a mile to Highland Lake. This lovely lake has a sandy beach along its NE shore, perfect for swimming on a warm sunny day. And the view south is tremendous. (The trail heading east from Highland Lake is the new Spear Lake trail. This 2 mile section of new trail hasn't been traveled by the author but is shown on the map as drawn by the Forest Service. This trail is reported to be moderate with several switchbacks as it follows the south slope of a ridge above Kearny Lake Reservoir.)

The trail south from Highland Lake descends moderate-steep for a mile to Kearny Creek. The waterfall across the creek comes from Penrose Canyon, accessible by climbing up beside the falls. From there it is possible to hike all the way to the cirques just east of and 1,900' below Black Tooth Mountain.

From the waterfall, follow Kearny Creek upstream for 1 mile to Spear Lake. While the peaks south of here are attained only by technical climbs, the lakes, waterfalls, and snowfields below them can be reached by hiking up the waterways. One pours into Spear Lake from Black Tooth to the south; the drainage from Five Fingers Canyon joins Kearny Creek about 0.5 mile SW of Spear.

Nearly a mile up the creek from Spear Lake, Exit Pass may allow a crossing to the west side of the divide. The approach from this side is very steep,

Innominate from Penrose Canyon.
Photo by JoAnn Emerson

over scree and boulders and the upper part is often covered with a snowdrift well into summer. This passage leads to the Cliff Lake Trail (p. 82) and a possible loop via Geneva Pass to where the account began, near the East Fork of Big Goose Creek.

(The next-shortest passage to the west side involves backtracking north from Highland Lake to the SW edge of Highland Park, then boulder-hopping up the bowl to the NW. At the saddle just SW of peak "10,991", turn south, past peaks "11,370" and "11,760" to Rainbow Lake and the Cliff Lake Trail just west of Lake Eunice.)

Spear Lake. *Photo by Marcus Johnshoy*

The other trail from the NW corner of Highland Park is part of the Solitude Loop. It goes east to Willow Park Reservoir and to Elk Lake south of that. Head SE across the park to its eastern rim. (The trail beyond this point is overused and muddy and will be replaced by a trail to the SW, joining the Spear Lake Trail just east of Highland Lake.) Begin a moderate descent from the rim, first north then curving around to the south. Then level off and turn east, passing north of Lake Winnie in wet meadows. About 0.5 mile east of the lake, begin a moderate-steep passage down this ridge, the north lateral moraine of the Kearny Lake Glacier. Turn south and descend to where the Spear Lake Trail forks west. Kearny Lake Reservoir is 0.4 mile south.

The trail turns east at the earthen dam which in 1963 turned two natural lakes here into one reservoir. Look for signs hereabouts of past forest fires and the subsequent regrowth. From the reservoir it's all moderate-level hiking along the north side of Kearny Creek. After 3.5 miles cross on bridge and head SE up ridge another mile to Willow Park Reservoir.

At the reservoir the trail joins a jeep trail which circles the reservoir. Turn SW and go around the west shore. Cross South Piney Creek (bridge) near its inlet to the reservoir. (As the trail from here to Elk Lake is a wide and well-worn jeep trail on dry ridges, those with more time may prefer following South Piney Creek, walking on creek-side boulders and the dim trail to Frying Pan Lake. This valley is exquisite - deep, shady and verdant. From Frying Pan, a trail connects with the main jeep trail to Elk Lake.)

From the reservoir, the jeep trail begins a moderate-steep climb to the south for 3.3 miles, then turns west to cross the shallow Elk Creek. West of the creek the trail to Frying Pan Lake begins. Turn south along this slow-moving creek for another mile to a side-trail going SW to Cloud Peak Reservoir, Mead Lake and the deep cirques east of Cloud Peak. (Just south of this junction, side trail east ascends for 0.5 mile to Gem Lake.) Trail to Elk Lake continues south 0.5 mile to junction with trails coming from SE and SW. See p. 57 for continuation of trails south from Elk Lake.

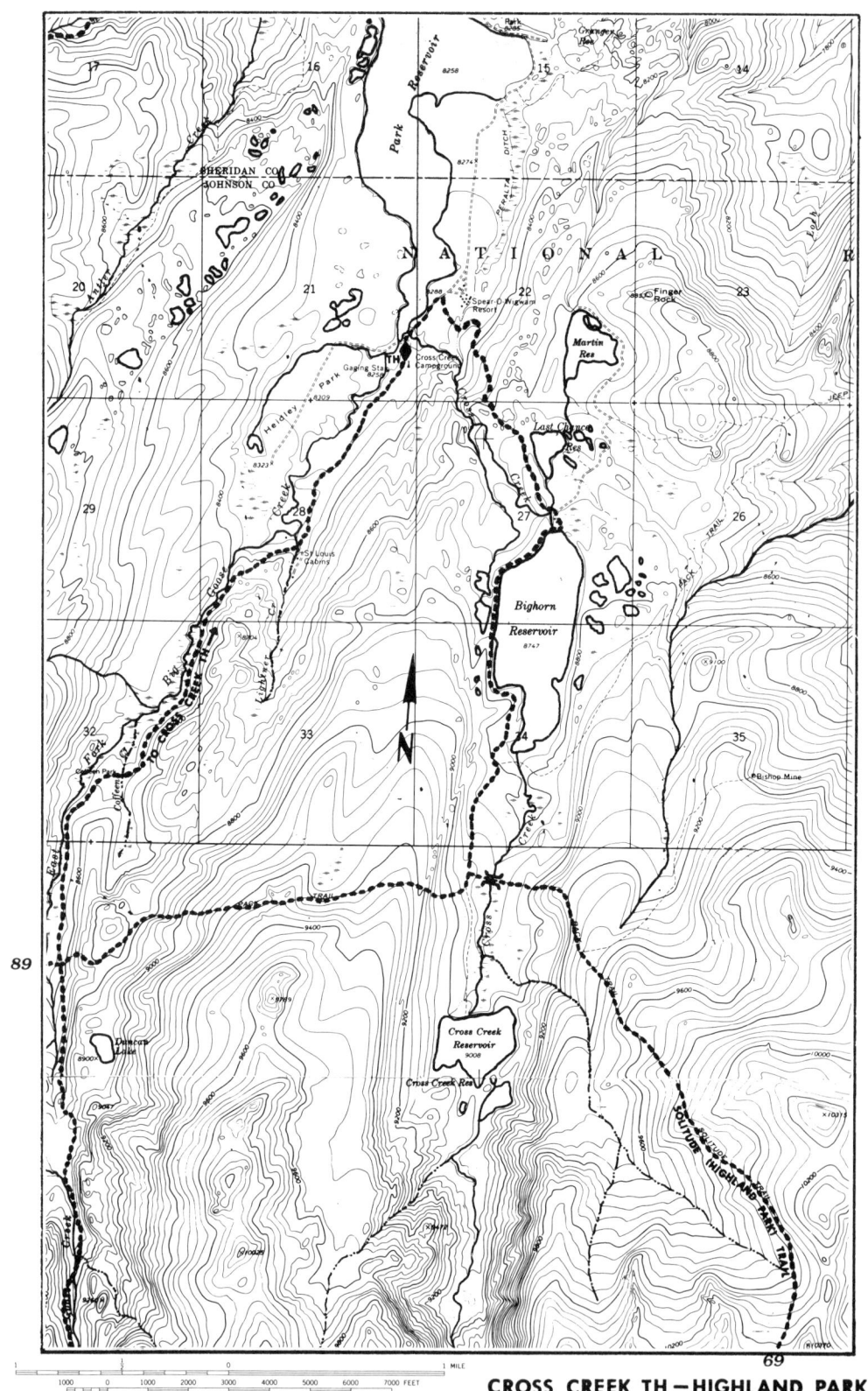

CROSS CREEK TH—HIGHLAND PARK

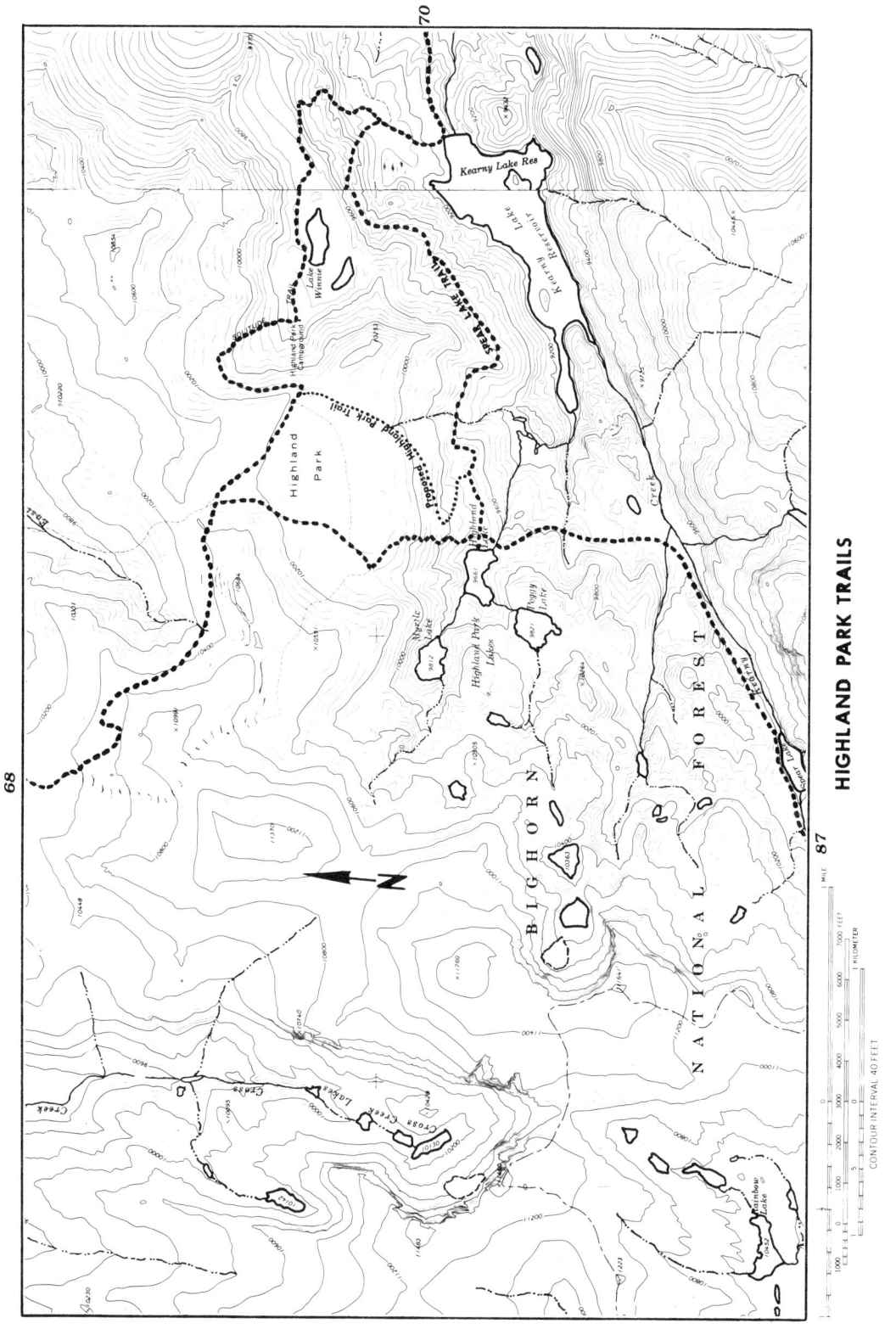

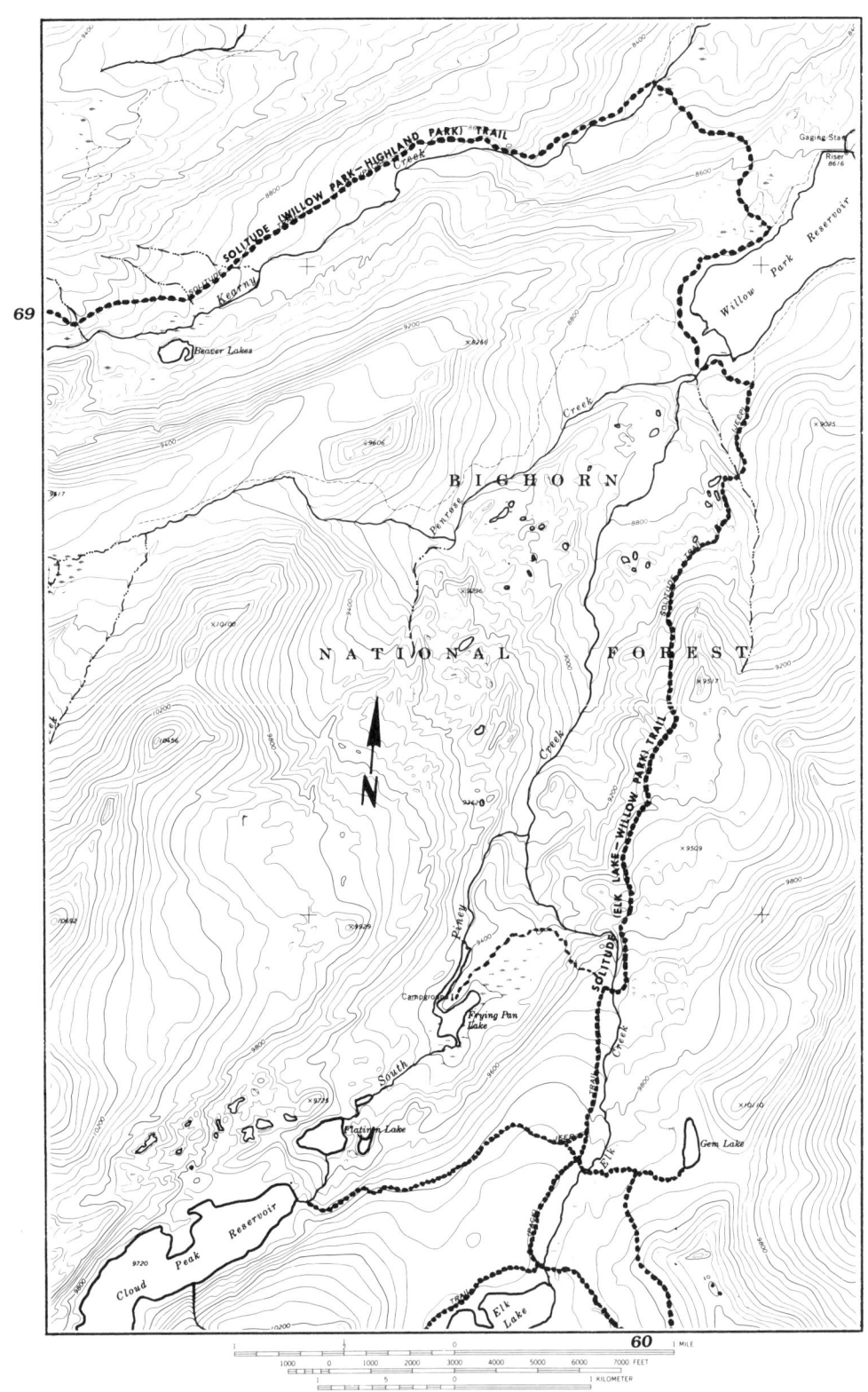

KEARNY CREEK — WILLOW PARK — ELK LAKE

Big Goose Trailhead to Geddes Lake

This is a non-loop trail covering a distance of 7 miles with an elevation gain of 2,700'. The trail to Geddes Lake follows Babione Creek and the rugged West Fork of Big Goose Creek. This trail has no designated trailhead. For those in automobiles, the Forest Service advises parking at the Big Goose Ranger Station. High-clearance, four wheel drive vehicles can go as far as the Babione Creek crossing at the south end of Big Goose Park.

Leave your vehicle at Big Goose Ranger Station, head south, crossing the Forest Service road and walk up the jeep trail. This trail heads south through the southern half of Big Goose Park. Walking through this park, hikers encounter junctions with two other jeep trails; bear to the right to stay on the main trail to Geddes Lake. After 1 mile, the trail leaves Big Goose Park and enters thick stands of lodgepole pine dropping down to a park just before Babione Creek. Southwest past the east edge of the park, hikers will find a junction with a trail heading SE up Antler Creek. Continue SW along south bank of Babione Creek. The trail is moderate-steep through lodgepole pine. The trail is now over what was once the east edge of the Dome Lake Glacier.

At the 4 mile point, cross Babione Creek to the north bank and continue climbing through timber west towards Weston Reservoir. The trail passes the south shore of Weston Reservoir and climbs moderately heading west. Hikers come upon a north-south junction on a ridge east of and above Heart Lake. The trail heading north leads to private property surrounding Dome Lake. The Forest Service advises that hikers are not allowed to enter or cross this private property. The trail south leads to Geddes Lake.

The trail climbs through timber and rounds the

east side of a knob before bending to the west. Continue south on the slope east of the West Fork of Big Goose Creek. Pass the east shore of Lake Mirage. The trail is moderate through light timber. Cross the West Fork of Big Goose Creek to its west bank and continue south to the NW shore of Geddes Lake. Boulder-strewn Elk Peak, the highest point in this area, is west of Geddes Lake.

From Geddes Lake, the trail is dim and not well maintained south to Lake Buffalo. The lake is 0.7 mile south of Geddes over a rocky, moderate-steep trail. The Forest Service maintains the trail only as far south as Geddes Lake.

GEDDES LAKE TRAIL

Twin Lakes Trailhead to Coney Lake

This non-loop trail covers a distance of 3.5 miles and represents an elevation gain of 700'. This is an ideal trek for those who don't have much time but who may want to spend one night in the wilderness. This might also be considered a good trail for children because the trail is not severe or strewn with boulders.

Park your vehicle at the large Twin Lakes Picnic Ground and proceed west up the service road located on the north side of picnic area. After 0.5 mile of easy walking, the trail crosses the east end of the Twin Lakes reservoir. The trail continues in cool, shady timber along the SE shore of the larger Twin Lake. The trail climbs gently for 1 mile through timber and bogs until reaching the east shore of the larger Stull Lake. The trail continues SW between the two Stull Lakes. Trail crosses a drainage (rock bridge) which connects the two lakes. From the larger Stull Lake, Coney Lake is 2 miles west.

West of this drainage the trail climbs sharply and enters the Primitive Area. From the Primitive Area boundary marker, the trail continues west and undulates over rocky, timbered terrain. The trail is well marked and easy to follow.

One mile west of the Primitive Area boundary, hikers reach the east shore of Coney Lake. Flat camping areas are available along the east shore of the lake. Coney Lake is clear, rocky and scenic. The trail terminates on the east shore of Coney Lake. After camping, fishing and exploring, hikers can return to Twin Lakes via the same route.

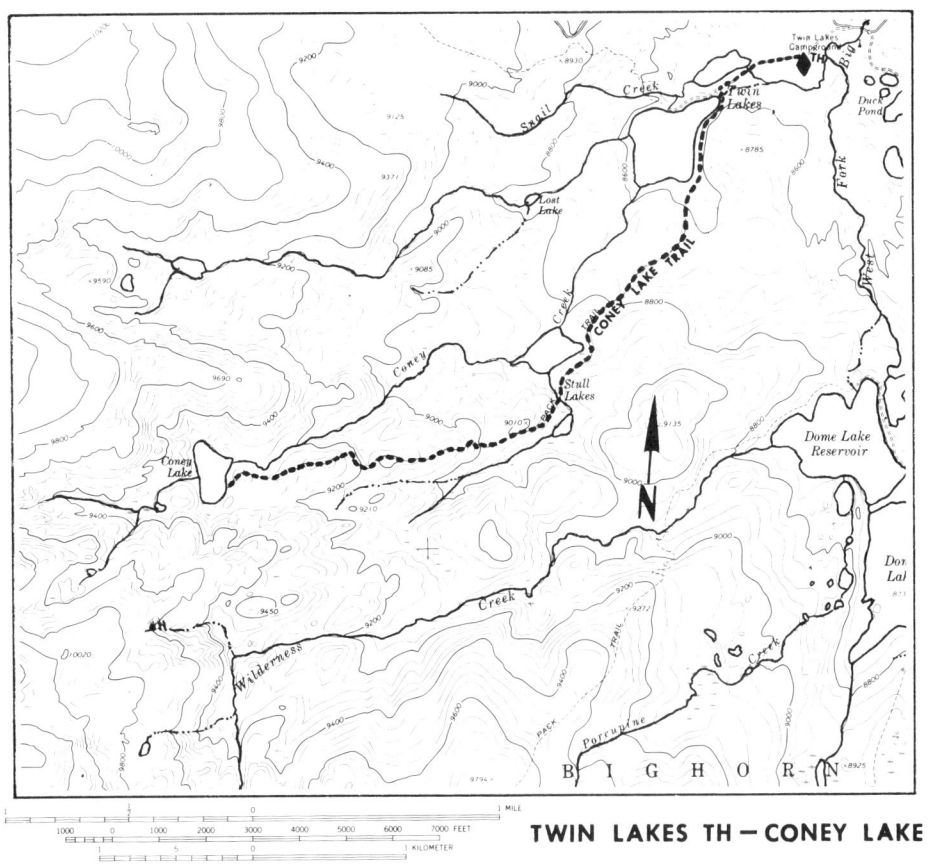

TWIN LAKES TH – CONEY LAKE

Lower Paint Rock Trailhead to Cliff Lake, Lake Geneva and Edelman Trailhead

These 21 miles of trail are described as a loop because the trail begins and ends at trailheads only 1.5 miles apart With trailheads so close together, it's possible to make the loop with no backtracking. This narrative includes descriptions of side trails leading to Lake Solitude, the Cliff Lake Loop including Exit Pass, and the trail to Shell Lake.

This elliptical route follows the contours of at least four different drainages. The Bighorn Divide is crossed at Geneva Pass and Edelman Pass, where water sheds west to the Bighorn River or east to the Tongue or Powder Rivers - but eventually north to the Yellowstone River and on to the sea. Most of this loop is within the Primitive Area; the eastern portion is part of the Solitude Trail system.

Those who take this route will see terrain ranging from heavy timber to high, windswept passes with spectacular vistas. These trails are not heavily used. Good water should be available at several points.

The two trailheads, Edelman and Lower Paint Rock Lakes, are located outside the western border of the Primitive Area. We begin this loop from the Lower Paint Rock Lakes Trailhead. Lake Geneva is 12.5 miles NE with an elevation gain of 1,700'. Good water might be available at a point 3 miles east of the trailhead.

Leaving the large parking area and corrals of Lower Paint Rock, proceed east across Trout Creek and into the heavy timber. You are on the North High Park Trail. Pass through a gate, close it, and climb into timber. The well-marked trail is moderate, making several ridge crossings in the first mile.

After 2 miles, descend a grass covered slope to Sheep Creek (bridge) then climb over ridge east of Sheep Creek. Descend to Firebox Creek (bridge) 3 miles from trailhead. The water in Firebox should be good for drinking, as the creek springs forth 0.5 mile north of the trail.

Continue east for 0.7 of a mile then turn south, down to Teepee Pole Flats. The Flats is a long, narrow meadow. At the east end of the Flats the trail forks: the route heading SW leads to Lake Solitude (side trail A); the trail east is to Cliff Lake and Lake Geneva.

Continue east through the meadows along North Paint Rock Creek. After 1.5 miles, re-enter timber and ascend moderately until crossing the creek on a log foot bridge. Climb into timber south of the creek, then descend to a clearing where the well-marked trail junction is located. Cliff Lake (side trail B) is 1.5 miles east. Lake Geneva is 5.5 miles north. Just south of this junction a spring can be found a short climb up the talus slope.

The trail north is moderate as it winds up the north North Paint Rock drainage. One-half mile north of junction, cross creek (rock bridge) and follow west bank of creek past several small lakes. After 2.5 miles, trail is joined by Cliff Lake Trail coming from SE (see side trail B). The drainage is narrower now as you pass east of Robin Lake, a small alpine (i.e. no timber) lake.

The North Paint Rock drainage was once beneath the massive Paint Rock Glacier. Evidence of glacial action is minimal in this valley, one of the few in the Bighorns where a glacier left no cirque at the head of its glaciated valley.

The trail continues north from Robin Lake 0.5 mile to Geneva Pass. The landscape here is predominantly granite rock, with sparse vegetation squeezing a living from cracks or the rare horizontal surface. It is possible to walk for miles to the east or west without touching 'ground' - just rocks, lichens or snow.

Cross high, (10,200') windswept Geneva Pass and descend north into the valley of East Fork Big Goose Creek. The head of this valley is narrow, talus-lined and boulder-strewn - the work of the Middle Finger of Lighter Glacier, which reached some 9 miles to the north.

View north, from Geneva Pass. *Photo by Ken Melius*

One-fourth mile north of Geneva Pass, look for the tailings of an abandoned mine just above the trail. Wooden trusses decay where the miners left them. In this colorful, highly mineralized area, miners were looking for gold; they found only fools' gold. Good water should be available from the waterfall SE of the mine.

Follow the creek down through the subalpine zone to Crystal Lake. The lake is in a beautiful circular basin with granite walls to the west and timber on the north. Pass east of the lake and, as you descend on the steep trail, watch for openings that allow views of Lake Geneva and the valley north.

From the pass it's 2.5 miles to Lake Geneva with its flat, wet meadow just upstream - a characteristic of many lakes in this range. Follow the east shore of the lake for 0.5 mile. Descent is moderate-steep north from Geneva. Here the creek is fast and noisy, dropping some 350' in 1 mile. Cross the creek after 1 mile, then again 1 mile farther in a flat boggy area. From here the 1 mile descent to the junction is moderate-steep.

Lake Geneva and view SW to Bighorn Divide.
Photo by JoAnn Emerson

Just before the junction, good water flows off the ridge to the east in several places. Duncan Lake is east, just over the ridge. The junction is with trails going east to Highland Park (p. 61); north through Coffeen Park to Cross Creek Trailhead (p. 61) and SW over Edelman Pass to Edelman Trailhead.

Edelman Pass is 3.7 miles from the junction. Follow trail west, crossing Big Goose Creek. Turn SW and follow west bank of Edelman Creek. Trail (now the Edelman Trail) is a moderate rise for 1 mile to Devils Lake junction. (This trail crosses creek then turns south around ridge (note old cabin) ascending moderate-steep for 1 mile to Devils Lake; a round lake with a rocky edge on the south and east, and a slow, grassy drainage therefrom.)

From the Devils Lake junction, the trail heads west then south along the base of the steep ridge west of the creek. The trail is rough with loose rocks and apparently sees little use. It is moderate-steep for 0.7 of a mile before crossing Edelman Creek to its east bank. Here the creek slows in winding through wet meadows. The trail is level for 0.5 mile, passing old dried-up lake beds. These present the near-climax stage of succession - from lake to meadow to forest - as the climate has become warmer and drier in the centuries since the glaciers receded.

Where the trail skirts a large bog rimmed with dead trees, cross a small creek that flows from Thayer Lake just to the east. Soon after, cross Edelman Creek to its west side. The ascent is steep-moderate for the 1.5 miles to the pass. Spruce and fir tower 80'-100' overhead with many great logs fallen in their midst. After 0.5 mile recross the creek (note the foundation and charred remains of a cabin just east of the trail).

The trail is ill-defined for the last 0.5 mile. Stay on the east side of the creek, crossing several side channels and lush springs with good drinking water. Rock-hopping is the rule until reaching the pass.

From Edelman Pass, descend to the bowl holding Emerald Lake. Follow the west shore of Emerald where the trail becomes better defined. The trail heading NW from the west rim of the lake leads to Shell Lake (side trail C).

Three glaciers extended from the Emerald Lake area: South Medicine Lodge to the SW, the Great Shell Creek Glacier to the NW and the Lighter Glacier on the north.

Take the trail heading SW out of the bowl towards

Emerald Lake. Edelman Pass, left of center.
Photo by Ken Melius

Edelman Trailhead, 4.5 miles distant. The trail descends moderately through the rocky upper reaches of Medicine Lodge Creek, following its west side for 2 miles before crossing.

The valley broadens and the trail is level-moderate as it heads SW through Edelman Park. Here the trail becomes a jeep road. Near the south end of the park, cross one minor drainage, then walk up the jeep trail to Edelman Trailhead. Lower Paint Rock Lakes Trailhead is 1.5 miles south on a Forest Service road.

SIDE TRAILS

A. LAKE SOLITUDE: This 3.5 mile section of the Solitude Trail connects Teepee Pole Flats (North High Park Trail) with Lake Solitude SE and a trail south to Battle Park. This connection is mostly the ascent and descent of a ridge, an elevation gain of 800'.

From the junction at the east end of Teepee Pole Flats, take Solitude Trail SW crossing North Paint Rock Creek. Enter timber on south side of the Flats and climb a steep trail with several switchbacks until topping Poacher Ridge. Level trail now passes the NW shore of lily-covered Sheepherder Lake. As you walk through this area, look east to spot Nunatak Point. In glacial terminology, a nunatak is a point or mountain which remains above and is surrounded by a glacier, in this case the huge Paint Rock Glacier.

Continue on the flat ridge top passing Poacher Lake near its east shore. This shallow lake is located in a large bog surrounded with pine. From the lake, trail bends east descending through areas of meadow and bog. Leave the meadows, climb into the timber, top a ridge and begin the steep descent to Paint Rock Creek.

After crossing a drainage (bridge) approach Paint Rock Creek and head east, soon coming to a junction (fork west leads down main Paint Rock Creek to Hyatt Cow Camp on the western slope of the Bighorns). The Solitude Trail continues east a short distance before turning south and crossing the creek (wade or use rock bridge).

Once up the south bank, the trail forks (trail SW leads to Grace Lake and Battle Park). From this fork the Solitude Trail heads east, reaching Lake Solitude after 1 mile.

B. CLIFF LAKE LOOP: This loop trail leads from the Solitude Trail to the well-named Cliff Lake and beyond, into the spectacular alpine territory west of The Bighorn Divide. From here it is possible to cross to the east side - Spear Lake and Highland Park - via Exit Pass; or circle back to the north and rejoin the Solitude Trail. The trail is moderate, 4.5 miles in length and gains 700' in elevation.

From the junction follow the waterway up. In several places good water runs off the slope to the south. Cross the creek and stay on the open, dry north side all the way to Cliff Lake. Pass through beautiful meadows with fescue and needlegrass prominent. After 2 miles approach Cliff Lake. This lake is in two levels, separated by a dam of boulders: west lake is smaller, shallow, and grassy; east is rock-rimmed, long and windswept. Both levels reflect 600' cliffs to the south.

Continue east from Cliff Lake along the creek. To the south can be seen the drainage from Crater Lakes. Here it is possible to make a side-trip to these remote lakes in their deep cirque.

Within 0.5 mile from Cliff the trail turns north to Lake Eunice, passing huge boulders south of Eunice. Travel is rather uninhibited in this lofty country. Passage north to Rainbow Lake and beyond to the great cirques of Cross Creek Lakes is readily made (see map, p. 69). By going north around the east side of the cirques and past peak "11,760", it's possible to join up with the Highland Park Trail to the NE. Take care in this area with its delicate vegetation, walking on rocks as much as possible; use a stove for cooking (no fires).

A shorter but more difficult and precarious route to the Highland Park area is through Exit Pass, a route not recommended for the novice or solo traveler. To reach this pass, continue east along the creek where the Cliff Lake Trail turns north to Lake Eunice. This brings you to Lake Elsa. Pass NW of the lake then bear north to get around the steep ridge NE of the lake. Turn SE above this ridge, then east up the bowl to Exit Pass. From here a 0.7 mile scramble south over boulders brings you to Panorama Point - stupendous!

East from the pass is where it gets difficult: a steep descent on boulders. Snowbanks which catch on this lee side are impossible to avoid most of the year. With backpacks you may find it helpful to lower the packs ahead of you on ropes for better balance. Pick a route carefully from the pass, (if the snowbanks at the pass look too precarious, descend a waterchute (crack) just north of the snowbanks) generally NE towards some grassy areas on the north side of the valley. Once down, proceed along Kearny Creek to Spear Lake.

For the rest of the Cliff Lake Loop, go north along Lake Eunice's west shore. Near NW edge turn to the NW (where a fork goes north to Rainbow Lake). From here on, views of the majestic peaks to the SE may be had. The trail passes ponds and bogs, then over a ridge into the North Paint Rock drainage.

Dolerite (mafic) dike NW of Cliff Lake.
Photo by M. Melius.

On the ridge look NW at a dark vein in the rock, running several miles east-west. This is a dike of dolerite, one of many in the Bighorns. The material is harder than the surrounding granite, so it often forms prominent ridges as it erodes, such as on Black Tooth Mountain.

From the ridge the trail winds down west to rejoin the Solitude Trail, leading north to Geneva Pass or back south 2 miles to the junction where the Cliff Lake Trail began.

C. SHELL LAKE: From the west shore of Emerald Lake, Shell Lake is 2.3 miles NW with a gradual descent in elevation of 700'. Shell Lake is a scenic lake surrounded by timber and meadow. Little Shell Lake is just north of the larger lake.

Head NW from Emerald through the subalpine area passing the three Lakes of the Rough. The huge Shell Creek Glacier formed in this wide canyon. The glacier was 14 miles long and covered 35 square miles.

Follow the north bank of Shell Creek as the creek weaves its way through sparse stands of spruce and fir. Pass through a marsh 0.5 mile east of Shell Lake then descend to north shore of Shell Lake. The lake is outside the Primitive Area. This trail offers no loop. Hikers are advised to backtrack to Emerald Lake. A dim trail climbs south out of the Shell Lake area, then SE over Dutch Oven Pass, but this trail receives no maintenance, is hard to find, and the pass is a difficult climb - especially with packs.

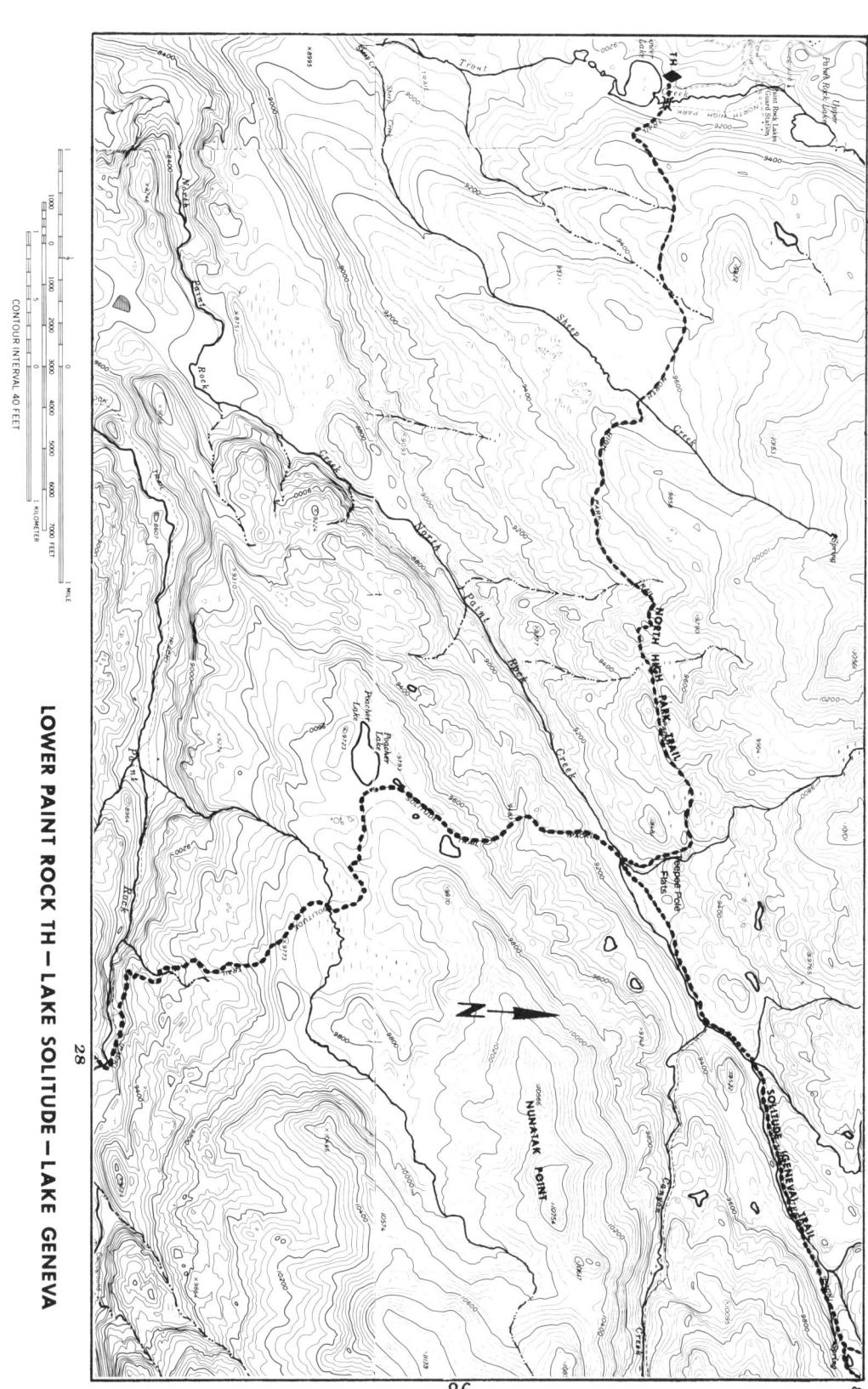

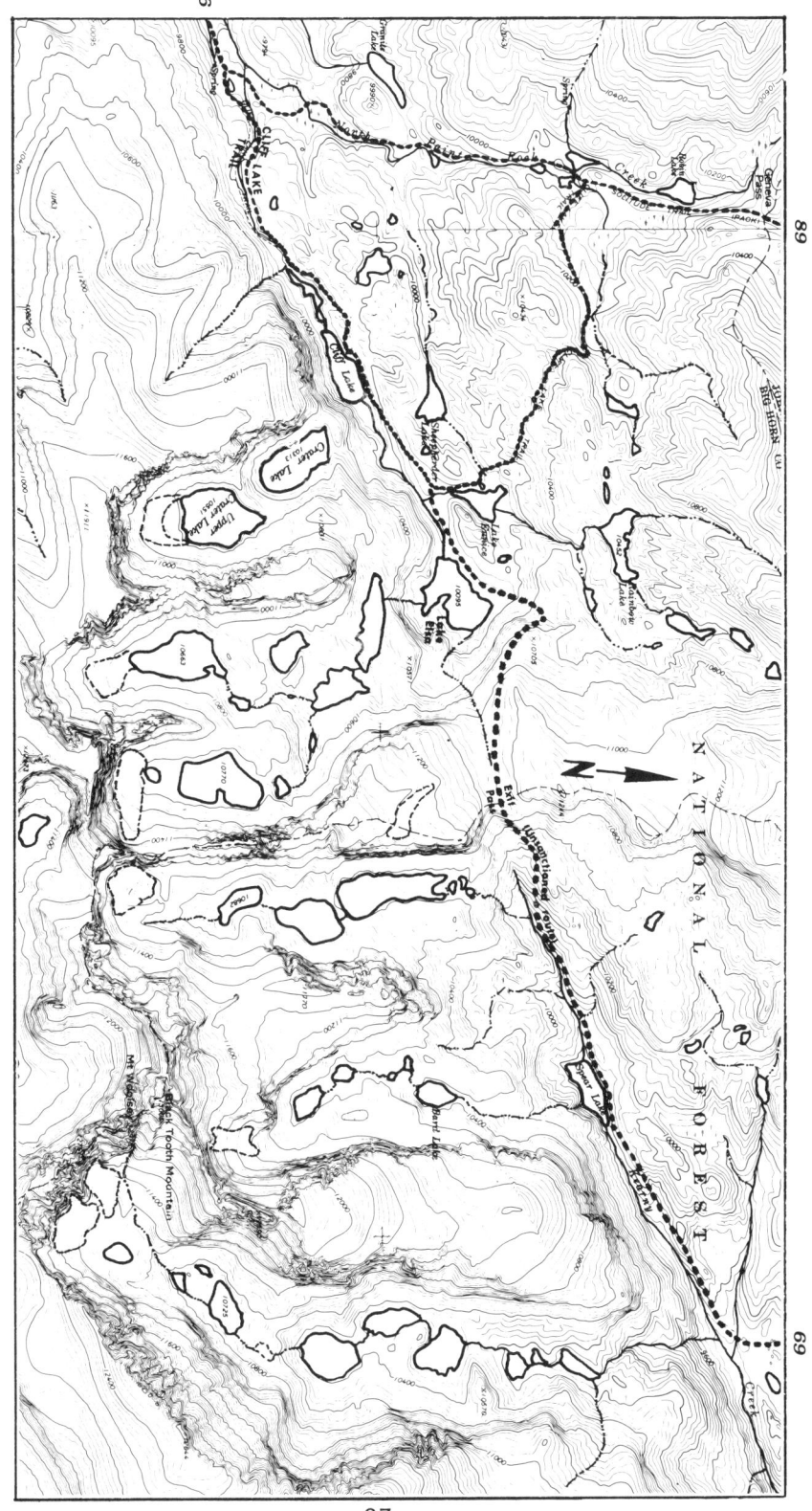

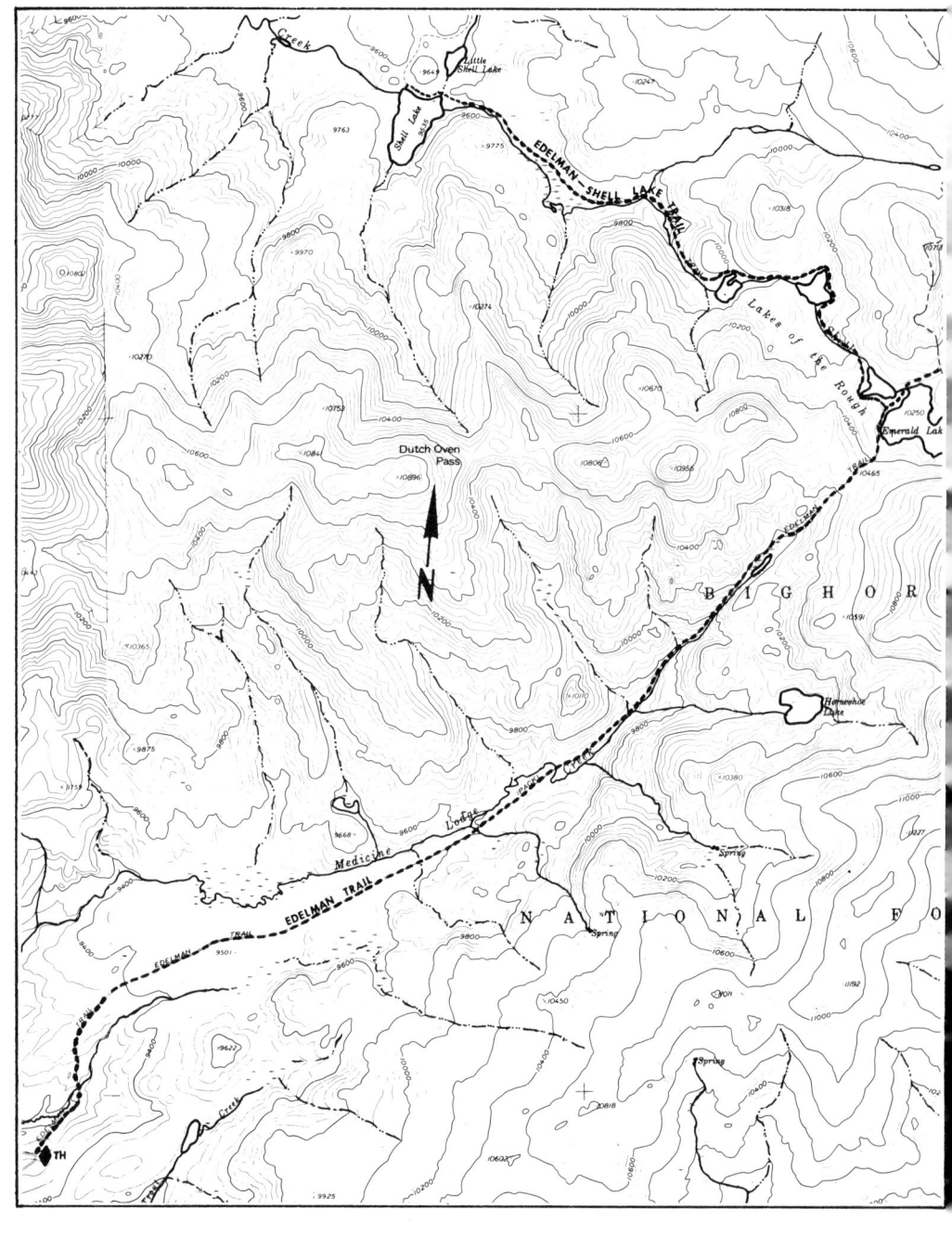

EDELMAN TH — EMERALD LAKE — SHELL LAKE

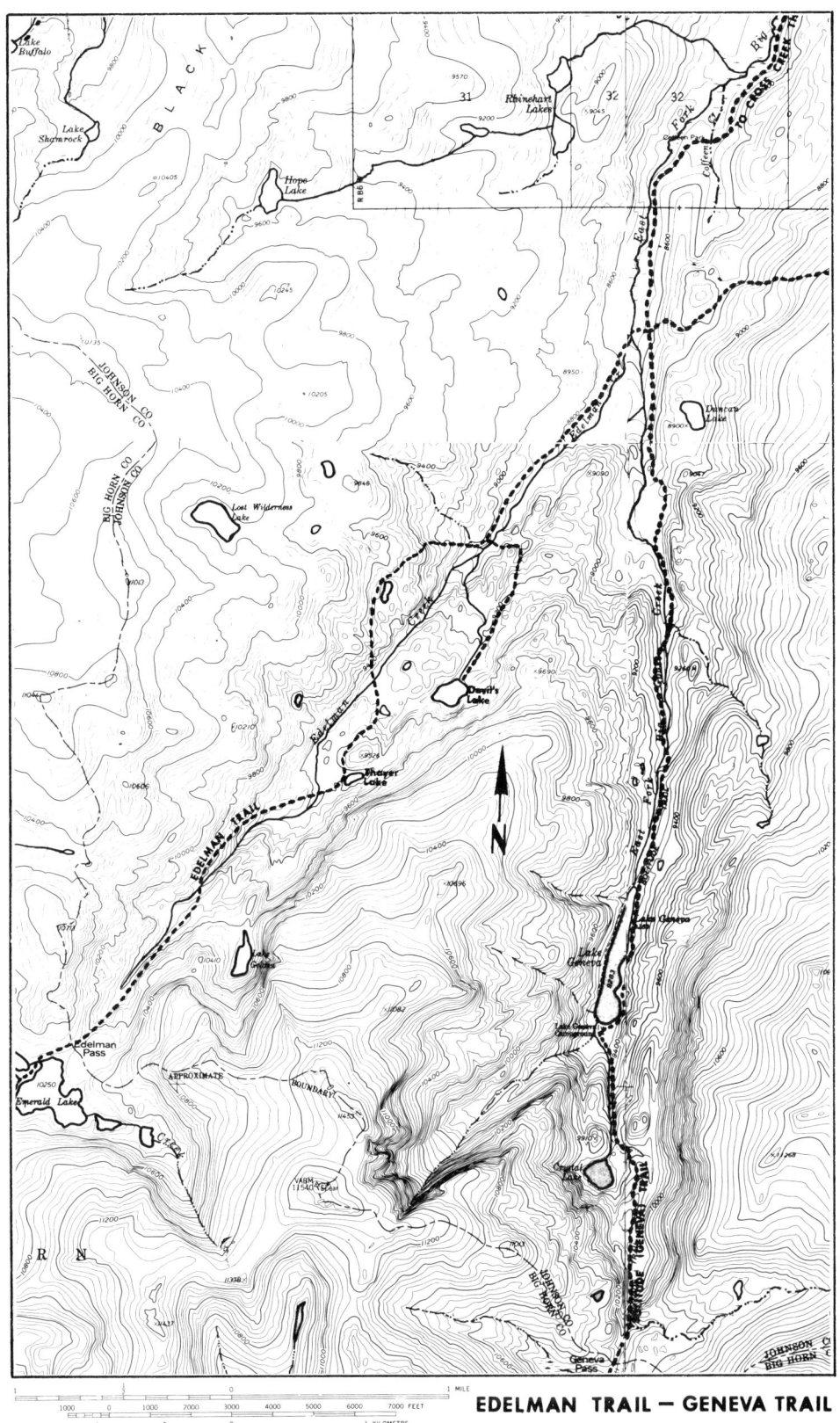

EDELMAN TRAIL — GENEVA TRAIL

Loop Routes

The following are suggested loop routes for travel in various parts of the Primitive Area. Included are routes that originate and end at or near the same trailhead. Time elements (Day 1, Day 2) are general guidelines; actual travel time from point to point may vary with the individual or group.

Using some routes involves off-trail travel. If traveling off-trail, carry the appropriate 7.5 minute topographic maps and make sure you're properly equipped. When planning a loop trip, consider alternate routes in the event trails or passes are blocked by snow or fallen timber.

Day 1 Battle Park TH to Grace Lake.
Day 2 Grace Lake to Lake Solitude.
Day 3 Lake Solitude to Mistymoon Lake.
Day 4 Mistymoon to Lily Lake.
Day 5 Lily Lake to Paint Rock TH then 1 mile to Battle Park TH.

An unhurried trip with some steep sections. 4 to 5 days minimum.

Day 1 Hunter Corrals TH to Seven Brothers via Buffalo Park.
Day 2 Seven Brothers (side trip to Angeline).
Day 3 Seven Brothers to Soldier Park via Trail Park.
Day 4 Soldier Park to Hunter Corrals.

Hunter Corrals to Seven Brothers is the steepest section of this loop. An unrushed trip, popular with horse packers. 3 to 4 days minimum.

Day 1 Hunter Corrals TH to Soldier Park.
Day 2 Soldier Park to Medicine Cabin Park.
Day 3 Medicine Cabin to Mistymoon Lake.
Day 4 Mistymoon to West Tensleep Lake.
Day 5 West Tensleep to the upper reaches of Middle Tensleep Creek.
Day 6 Middle Tensleep to Seven Brothers via Lake Angeline.
Day 7 Seven Brothers to Hunter Corrals via Buffalo Park.

A long, strenuous trek involving off-trail travel. Plan carefully. 7 days minimum.

Day 1 Cross Creek TH to Upper Highland Park.
Day 2 Highland to Spear Lake.
Day 3 Spear to Cliff Lake via Exit Pass.
Day 4 Cliff to Lake Geneva.
Day 5 Geneva to Cross Creek TH via Coffeen Park.

A long loop with steep sections, should be attempted later in summer when Exit Pass is less snow-laden. 5 days minimum.

Day 1 Edelman TH to north of Edelman Pass.
Day 2 Edelman Pass to Upper Highland Park.
Day 3 Highland to Spear Lake.
Day 4 Spear to Cliff Lake via Exit Pass.
Day 5 Cliff Lake to Teepee Pole flats.
Day 6 Teepee Pole to Lower Paint Rock TH then 1.5 miles north to Edelman TH.

A lengthy route, steep in places. 6 days minimum.

Wildlife

Wildlife occurring in the Cloud Peak Primitive Area include moose, elk, mule and whitetail deer, bighorn sheep, mountain lion, black bear, fox and coyote.
Smaller animals include snowshoe hare, yellowbelly marmot, porcupine and squirrel.

Fishing

The Cloud Peak Primitive Area offers fishing in 256 lakes and 49 miles of fishing streams. Trout species found in the Primitive Area include; California Golden (found in high altitude lakes and streams), Native Cutthroat, Eastern Brook, German Brown, Mackinaw, and Rainbow. Grayling are present in several lakes in the Primitive Area.
The fishing season is open all year throughout the Primitive Area. The State of Wyoming offers several types of fishing licenses: resident fishing license - $7.50, nonresident fishing license - $30.00 and tourist five-day license - $10.00. These licenses can be purchased in most sporting goods stores throughout Wyoming.
The following is an alphabetical listing of fishing lakes and reservoirs located in or near the Cloud Peak Primitive Area. Abbreviations for the fish species found in each body of water are listed to the right of each entry.

Cutthroat = Ct   Mackinaw = Mk   Rainbow = Rw
Brook = Bk   Golden = Go
Brown = Bw   Grayling = Gr

Bard Lake - Ct
Beaver Lake - Bw
Bighorn Reservoir - Bk, Bw, Rw
Brown Bear Lake - Ct, Rw
Bruce Lake - Bw
Calvin Lake - Ct
Christine Lake - Ct
Cliff Lake - Bw

Cloud Peak Reservoir - Ct, Rw
Coney Lake - Bk
Crater Lake - Mk
Cross Creek Reservoir - Bk, Bw, Rw
Crystal Lake - Rw
Deer Lake - Bk
Devil's Lake - Bk, Mk
Duncan Lake - Bw
Elephant Head Lake - Go
Emerald Lake - Bk
Firehole Lakes - Ct, Bk, Go, Mk, Rw
Flat Iron Lake - Bk, Ct, Rw
Florence Lake - Ct
Fortress Lakes - Co
Frying Pan Lake - Bk, Ct, Rw
Geddes Lake - Bk
Grace Lake - Bk
Granite Lake - Bk, Rw
Gunboat Lake - Go
Highland Park Lake - Bk, Rw
Hope Lake - Ct, Rw
Horseshoe Lake - Rw
Kearny Lake - Bk, Bw, Mk, Rw
Lake Angeline - Ct
Lake Buffalo - Bk
Lake Elsa - Bk
Lake Geneva - Bk, Mk
Lake Golden - Bk, Co
Lake Helen - Bk
Lake Marion - Bk, Bw, Rw
Lake Solitude - Bk, Ct, Mk
Lakes of the Rough - Ct
Lame Deer Lake - Bw, Rw
Lily Lake - Bk, Gr
Long Lake - Ct, Mk
Loomis Lake - Ct
Lost Lake - Ct
Lost Twin Lake (lower) - Rw
Lower Frozen Lake - Go
Lower Medicine Lodge Lake - Rw
Lower Paint Rock Lake - Bk
Lower Poacher Lake - Gr
Lower Rainbow Lake - Bk
Lower Shell Lake - Ct, Bk
Magdelene Lake - Ct, Rw
Martin Reservoir - Bk, Bw, Rw
MayBelle Lake - Ct
McLain Lake - Ct
Mead Lake - Ct
Middle Paint Rock Lake - Bw, Rw
Mirror Lake - Bk, Mk, Rw
Mistymoon Lake - Bk
Mud Lake - Bk
Myrtle Lake - Go
North Paint Rock Lake - Bk, Rw
Old Crow Lake - Bk, Bw, Ct, Go, Mk, Rw
Peggy Lake - Bk
Poacher Lake - Gr
Powell Lakes - Ct
Rainbow Lake - Bk
Rhinehart Lakes - Bk, Ct, Rw
Ringbone Lake - Ct, Gr
Robin Lake - Bk
Romeo Lake - Splake
Sawmill Lake - Bw
Sawtooth Lakes - Rw
Seven Brothers Lakes - Ct, Mk, Rw
Sheepherder Lake - Bk
Shell Lake - Bk
Sherd Lake - Ct
South Fork Ponds - Bk, Bw, Rw
South Piney Lakes - Ct
Spear Lake - Bk
Stull Lake - Bk, Bw, Rw
Thayer Lake - Bk
Triangle Lake - Bk
Trigger Lake - Ct, Rw
Twin Lakes - Ct, Bk, Bw
Upper Medicine Lodge Lake - Rw
Upper Paint Rock Lake - Bk
West Tensleep Lake - Ct, Bk, Rw
Weston Reservoir - Bk, Gr
Willow Lake - Ct, Gr, Splake
Willow Park Reservoir - Ct, Bk, Rw

Bird Life

This list of bird species* includes species which are abundant, common or fairly common on the Bighorn National Forest. Bird life listed below might be found in the Primitive Area.

Audubon's Warbler
Bald Eagle
Bohemian Waxwing
Brewer's Sparrow
Brown Thrasher
Calliope Hummingbird
Cassin's Finch
Chipping Sparrow
Common Flicker
Common Nighthawk
Dipper
Downy Woodpecker
Evening Grosbeak
Fox Sparrow
Golden Eagle
Gray-crowned Rosy Finch
Gray Jay
Great Horned Owl
Hairy Woodpecker
Horned Lark
Least Flycatcher
Lewis' Woodpecker
Mallard
Mountain Chickadee
Myrtle Warbler
Orange-crowned Warbler
Oregon Junco
Ovenbird
Pine Siskin
Red-breasted Nuthatch
Red-tailed Hawk
Rock Wren
Ruby-crowned Kinglet
Rufous Hummingbird
Swainson's Hawk
Swainson's Thrush
Townsend's Solitaire
Tree Sparrow
Tree Swallow
Turkey Vulture
Violet-green Swallow
Water Pipit
Western Tanager
White-crowned Sparrow
White-throated Swift
Wilson's Warbler
Yellow-bellied Sapsucker

*Source: Tongue Ranger District, U.S.D.A. Forest Service. From the collection of sightings by Platt H. Hall, Tom Kessinger, Helen Downing and others, 1966 to 1980. Edited by Helen Downing.

Resources

U. S. Forest Service Offices

Buffalo Ranger District
381 N. Main St.
Buffalo, Wyoming 82834
(307) 684-7981

Forest Supervisor's Office
1969 S. Sheridan Ave.
Sheridan, Wyoming 82801
(307) 672-0751

Medicine Wheel Ranger District
142 East 3rd, P.O. Box 367
Lovell, Wyoming 82431
(307) 548-6541

Paint Rock Ranger District
1220 N. 8th, P.O. Box 831
Greybull, Wyoming 82426
(307) 765-4435

Tensleep Ranger District
2009 Big Horn Ave.
Worland, Wyoming 82401
(307) 347-8291

Tongue Ranger District
1969 S. Sheridan Ave.
Sheridan, Wyoming 82801
(307) 672-0751

County Sheriff Offices

Big Horn County (Basin)   (307) 568-2324
Johnson County (Buffalo)   (307) 684-5581
Sheridan County (Sheridan)   (307) 672-3453
Washakie County (Worland)   (307) 347-2242

The following 7.5 minute topographic quadrangle maps (USGS) encompass the Cloud Peak Primitive Area.

Cloud Peak
Dome Lake
Hunter Mesa
Lake Angeline
Lake Helen

Lake Solitude
Park Reservoir
Shell Lake
Spanish Point
Willow Park Reservoir

U. S. Forest Service recreation maps of the Bighorn National Forest are available from Forest Service offices for $1.00.

The Bighorn range is located in north central Wyoming near the Wyoming-Montana border. Interstate Highway 90 passes the eastern slope of the Bighorns. U.S. 14 and 14A are the major east-west highways through the northern portion of the range; U.S. 16 is an east-west highway through the southern part of the range.

Sheridan, located east of the range on I-90, is the largest city in the area. Sheridan offers daily commercial airline service. Commercial passenger bus service is available to the cities of Buffalo and Sheridan on the east side of the range and Greybull, Lovell and Worland on the west side of the Bighorns.

Index

altitude sickness, 12
American War Dads, 54
animals, pack, 34, 39
animals, wild, 14, 45
Ant Hill, 57, 58

Bald Ridge, 26, 33
Big Goose Ranger Station, 19, 20, 71
Bighorn Basin, 23, 49
Bighorn Peak, 43
Bighorn Reservoir, 61, 62
Black Tooth, 62, 64, 85
Buffalo Back, 62
Buffalo Park, 45, 50
Bureau of Reclamation, 23

Cheyenne, 4
Chill Lakes, 43
Cloud Peak, 25, 27, 29, 31, 35, 36, 54, 57, 58, 67
Cloud Peak Reservoir, 5, 57, 67
Crater Lakes, 83
Cross Creek Reservoir, 61
Crow, 4
Crystal Lake, 78

Dacotah, 4
Darton Peak, 42, 43
Deer Lake, 51
Devil's Lake, 80
dolerite dike, 84
Dome Lake, 71
drinking water, 14, 22, 24, 26, 45, 57, 58, 61, 62, 76, 77, 79, 80, 83
Duck Creek Burn, 41
Duncan Lake, 79
Dutch Oven Pass, 85

Edelman Park, 81
Edelman Pass, 61, 62, 79, 80
Elk Mountain, 22
Emerald Lake, 80, 85
ethics, wilderness, 7
Exit Pass, 11, 64, 76, 82-83

felsenmeer, 63
Five Fingers, 62
forest fires, 6, 41, 67
Fortress Lakes, 54
Frozen Lakes, 47
Frying Pan Lake, 67

Garde, Peter, 50
Gem Lake, 57
glaciers, 3, 33, 41, 45, 56, 49, 50, 54, 58, 62, 66, 71, 77, 80, 82, 85
Grace Lake, 22, 26, 82
guard station, wilderness, 46
Gunboat Lake, 54

Hallelujah Peak, 62
Heart Lake, 71
Her Lake, 42
Hettinger, August, 50
Hunter Mesa, 45
Hunter Ranger Station, 19
Hyatt Cow Camp, 82
hypothermia, 12

Johnson, Carl, 50
Kearny Lake Reservoir, 61, 67
Lake Buffalo, 72
Lake Elsa, 83
Lake Eunice, 65, 83, 84
Lake Mirage, 72
Lake Winnie, 64, 66
Lakes of the Rough, 85
lightning, 13
Long Lake, 41, 42
Long Park, 22, 26
lost, if, 13
Lost Lake, 22
lumbering, 5

man-way, 11, 33, 38
Mead Lake, 57
Medicine Cabin Park, 52-53
Medicine Wheel, 4
mining, 4, 78
Mirror Lake, 38

Old Crow Lake, 42-43
Otter Lake, 42
overexertion, 12

Pacific Plate, 2
Panorama Point, 83
Penrose Peak, 57, 62
Poacher Lake, 23, 82
Powell Lakes, 52
President Cleveland, 5

Rainbow Lake, 65, 83, 84
Rainy Lake, 42
Red Grade Road, 20
Ringbone Lake, 42
Robin Lake, 77
Rocky Mountains, 2
routes, unsanctioned, 11, 38, 64, 82-83

Sawtooth Ridge, 62
Schoolhouse Park, 48
skiing, 8, 33
Soldier Park, 45, 50, 51, 57, 58
Solitude Trail, 5, 10, 30, 33, 57, 58, 66, 76, 82, 85
South Fork Ponds, 42
stream crossings, 13
striations, glacial, 34
Stull Lakes, 74

Teepee Pole flats, 77, 82
temperatures, average, 15
Thayer Lake, 80
Trail Park, 51, 57
Triangle Park, 51
Trigger Lake 42
Tyrell Ranger Station, 18

Webber Park, 48
Weston Reservoir, 71
Wilderness Basin, 24, 29, 30
Willow Lake, 42
wreckage, 25, 30

Yost Trail, 33

Annotated Bibliography

Bonney, Orrin H. and Lorraine G. *Field Book the Big Horn Range*, Chicago, The Swallow Press, Inc. 1977.
    A comprehensive trail guide for the Big Horn range including Cloud Peak Primitive Area. Extensive explanation of geology of the Big Horn range and history of the area. Includes description of technical climbing routes for all major peaks in the Big Horn range.

Wyoming. State Historical Society. *Rediscovering the Big Horns*, in cooperation with the Big Horn National Forest, U.S. Forest Service, 1976.
    A pamphlet depicting 75 years of ecological change throughout the Big Horn range. Locations photographed in 1900 by John G. Jack were photographed again in 1975. Photo comparisons illustrate the re-growth of burned or overgrazed areas.

Conner, J. F. *History of the Big Horn National Forest and Vicinity,* Laramie, University of Wyoming, 1940.
    Conner, a former supervisor of the Big Horn National Forest, described events occuring in or near the forest over a period of 60 years.

Murray, Robert A. *Multiple Use in the Big Horns, the Story of Big Horn National Forest*, USDA. 1980.
    A complete examination of forest use involving grazing, minerals, recreation and timber harvesting.

Darton, N. H. *Geology of the Big Horn Mountains*, Professional Paper No. 51, U.S.G.S. 1906.
    An interesting study of the geology and topography of the range. Also includes a detailed description of how glaciation affected the Big Horn range.